No Small Thing

NO SMALL THING

Ex-servicemen from British Southern Cameroons in WW 2: Royal West African Frontier Force, North Africa, Burma

ROBERT J. O'NEIL

The Crossroad Publishing Company
New York

The Crossroad Publishing Company
www.CrossroadPublishing.com

In continuation of our 200-year tradition of independent publishing, The Crossroad Publishing Company proudly offers a variety of books with strong, original voices and diverse perspectives. The viewpoints expressed in our books are not necessarily those of The Crossroad Publishing Company, any of its imprints or of its employees, executives, or owners. Although the author and publisher have made every effort to ensure that the information in this book was correct at press time, the author and publisher do not assume and hereby disclaim any liability to any party for any loss, damage, or disruption caused by errors or omissions, whether such errors or omissions result from negligence, accident, or any other cause. No claims are made or responsibility assumed for any health or other benefits.

Covor photo of Mr. Joseph Tepe Ndikum courtesy of Mr. Ndikum's daughter, Brigitte Nyada

Book design by The HK Scriptorium

Library of Congress Cataloging-in-Publication Data
available from the Library of Congress

ISBN 9780824595302 (paperback)
ISBN 9780824507572 (epub)

Books published by The Crossroad Publishing Company may be purchased at special quantity discount rates for classes and institutional use. For information, please e-mail sales@Crossroad Publishing.com.

Dedication

In memory of Professor Graham W. Irwin
Columbia University
Captain, 2nd/9th Armored Regiment, Australia,
World War II

Contents

Foreword

History aims at reporting events of the past to the present generation in the most lucid, authentic, and precise manner possible. It is also known that pictures don't lie and that a picture speaks a thousand words. In this volume, the author graphically engages the surviving Southern Cameroonian ex-servicemen, who like actors in a drama introduce themselves and vividly recount their individual experiences and encounters during World War II.

These are the incredible feats Father Robert O' Neil does in his publication: *No Small Thing*, a metaphorical title evoking the experiences elicited from some of his interlocutors attempting to recount the horrifying, gory battlefield spectacles they experienced, which defied description and efforts to recall. In so doing the author has concretized the highest standards of history set by the two most famous Greek historians: Herodotus, dubbed "The Father of History" by the Roman writer Cicero and admired by historians through the ages as the most credible source of information on the ancient world, and Thucydides, the other towering figure, who has been acknowledged as the father of "Scientific History" because of his claims to strict standards of impartiality, evidence-gathering, and the analysis of cause and effect in historical presentations.

In this book, the author demonstrably draws from his talents, integrity, and instincts as an experienced pastor and dedicated historian as elaborately established throughout this presentation.

However, if these introductory remarks set the compass for interpreting the narratives of the few surviving Southern Cameroons ex-servicemen who fought in World War II, many questions pop up begging for explanation and justification about what the so-called Cameroonian ex-servicemen were fighting and losing their lives for. Classically, wars are fought by a country or group of countries against opponents for specified objectives—economic, territorial, religious, political, civil, revenge, and ideological—none of which adequately applied to Southern Cameroons, which was in a state of flux.

Regardless of the flag, language, or creed, imperialism as exemplified in the case of Southern Cameroons downsized from the former German African empire, which until 1916 extended to Gabon, Congo, Central African Republic, Chad, and Nigeria is multilayered and exceedingly checquered and can never be justified. When to it are added the intrigues of the unilateral transfer of ownership after the defeat of Germany in the Second World War by the Allied Powers, the story becomes expressly intriguing and complicated. This is understandable because German influence was emblazoned in its very DNA, ingrained in its appellation, geography, economy, and the psyche of the people. Everything about Southern Cameroons engagement in the wars was miscalculated and bungled up. This explains why valiant and loyal conscripts absconded, some of whom even committed suicide. As it turned out in the interviews, very few of those who fought did so in accordance with Rudyard Kipling's romantic, poetic perspective of patriotism.

Colonized by Germany in 1884, it became a Franco-British condominium from 1915 to 1916, after the defeat of Germany in World War I, an experiment which collapsed barely after a year. It next floated in the air from 1916 to 1922, when it was administered as a League of Nations Mandated Territory under Britain. Interestingly, thereafter, despite its small size, it was causelessly mutilated yet into British Southern and British Northern Cameroons and placed under Southern and later Eastern Nigeria for fostering as a Trusteeship Territory of the United Nations with the capital at Enugu.

Sarcastically, it was often derisively referred to as the "colony of a region of a colony," and even worse, it was totally overrun and exploited by the populous Ibo ethnic group. Consequently, it tore away from the Eastern Region of Nigeria in protest and became a *Quasi-Region* in 1954. So, Southern Cameroonians were recruited in shadowy circumstances in both World Wars. Making things forever unpleasant for them, the British colonial administration paid scant attention to the socioeconomic and political administration of the territory, always treating it as a foster German territory of little socioeconomic and political consequence.

Indeed, Lord Lugard, the Governor General of Nigeria, considered Southern Cameroons as a burden and great liability, the reason for which it was continuously attached to and administered as an "appendage" of its Nigerian colony.

This was a bluff that the powerful German Nazi propaganda machine in the territory led by Herr Luppe readily called off, since the flourishing plantation economy and other investments that sustained the territory were entirely and firmly in German hands as the Second World War commenced. The people were assured that nothing would change, especially after early German victories in the war, the *Anschluss*, and the occupation of France by Nazi Germany, occasions loudly toasted at celebrations in Victoria and Tiko. The British were regarded as interlopers, and their hold on the Trust Territory was extremely tenuous.

Given these blurred circumstances, right or wrong, most of the conscripted ex-servicemen fought a sort of "proxy war" for reasons far removed from the lofty allusion to "proud nationalists" defending a vague British Empire, inscribed on epitaphs for their tombstones advanced by Rudyard Kipling. In *No Small Thing*, Fr. O'Neil deftly and innovatively uses the actors to tell their own stories, bridging history, geography, drama, and pictures to drive home the hard facts of historical narrative to the average reader. Essentially, he has set a new dimension for making history attractive, lively, and simple.

Professor Anthony Ndi
Cameroon Historian

Anthony Ndi is retired Associate Professor of History in Cameroon. He holds a B. Ed. (Hons) in History from the University of Ibadan and a Masters and a Ph.D. in African History from the School of Oriental and African Studies (SOAS) in London. He is also the associate editor of *Pan Tikar* and the author of books and articles including *Mill Hill Missionaries in Southern West Cameroon, 1922–1972; Southern West Cameroon Revisted*, (2 vols.); *The Golden Age of Southern Cameroons; and Reluctant Prince of the Mbot Kingdom*. Presently, he is working on a biography of Dr. John Ngu Foncha, onetime prime minister of Southern Cameroons and pioneer vice president of the Federal Republic of Cameroon.

Acknowledgments

The idea to write about the men from Southern Cameroons who served in the British Army in World War II began after reading an article on the subject in 1988. Dr. Yuusuf Caruso, since 1993 the African Studies librarian at Columbia University, mailed it to me in Cameroon. It was written by Anthony Ndi, who writes the Foreword for this book. Professor Ndi had contributed a chapter in a book about Africa and the Second World War. His subject was World War II and the Southern British Cameroons.

Without the help of Brigitte Ndikum Nyada and her husband, John, it is unlikely that the topic of these old soldiers made it to a book. Her father was Joseph Tepe Ndikum, whose picture is on the cover. She has been a ready contact concerning her late father for many years.

All the people mentioned in these pages deserve special thanks. In the UK the two archivists at the Mill Hill Missionaries in Freshfield, near Liverpool: the late Fr. Thomas O'Brien and currently Fr. Stephen Giles. Others include the late Fr. John Ball. Another is Fr. Bill Tollan.

In Cameroon the general superior of the Mill Hill Missionaries at the time, Fr. Maurice McGill, and the late archbishop of Bamenda, Paul Verdzekov, enabled me to work as a pastor while at the same time interviewing Cameroonian elders, including the old soldiers of this book.

Also in Cameroon, the late archivist Primus Forgwe, of the Buea Government archive, and Fr. Joseph Akem, who died in August 2024, helped many times to have access to information and people of interest; Mr. Philip Mbah of Bamenda has been a friend and regular contact in Cameroon for almost fifty years.

The suggestions of Emeritus Professor Hollis Lynch on an earlier book, *Born Under the Gun*, have been followed in *No Small Thing* as well. Early at Columbia, Professor Marcia Wright was an advisor for a study of Moghamo in Cameroon.

Others over the years have encouraged the pursuit of history and writing. All have passed on: Fr. Peter Logue of Mt. St. Bernard in the UK, who was guest master of the monastery in Mbengwi, Cameroon; Fr. James Lloyd of St. Paul's in Manhattan; and Professor Graham Irwin of Columbia University.

This book does not exist without the encouragement and support of publisher Gwendolin Herder of Crossroad. We also thank Maurya Horgan and

Paul Kobelski of the HK Scriptorium in Denver, Colorado, who helped to edit the text and design the book for publication.

Mr. Ben Forkwa is still at Mile 4 near Limbe with his family. Almost all of the interviews were done with his assistance, especially in remote areas, setting up an old tape recorder and transcribing the interviews into notebooks. We have known each other, along with Philip Mbah, from the 1970s, when the head-master of Enyoh Catholic primary school, Mr. George Ngati, brought them to my attention as manager of Catholic schools in Moghamo country.

There are family members who are part of this story: parents John and Pauline O'Neil; brother, Jack; and uncles: Fr. Tom O'Neil, Paul Sekelsky, and John Sekelsky. One aunt was also godmother, Margaret Holcomb. Aunt Peg was a nurse in World War II, serving in China and caring for wounded from Burma.

So many are involved in such a work. At the end I am grateful to the Lord for bringing me on this journey, however unlikely it has all been.

Preface

*Scholars who have talked to ex-servicemen and carefully recorded their memories of
an increasingly distant war when they fought for Britain have listened to their stories
of official neglect and unpaid benefits. "Lest we forget," the phrase of Rudyard Kipling
often inscribed on war memorials, is an apt one for the forgotten men of the African
colonial forces. . . . However, against this rather depressing note is the strong sense of
pride that many African ex-servicemen still hold as they look back on their wartime
service and experiences.*

David Killingray[1]

The *New York Times* of 11 November 2008 ran a piece about Veterans Day in
the United States. Veterans Day, it noted, began as an observance of the end of
fighting in World War I. The agreement to stop the war was called the Armistice. A day to mark it each year was called Armistice Day. It was to be a time of
prayer and reflection, remembering those who served in the Great War. Armistice Day was also called Poppy Day. It is now called Remembrance Day in Britain and the Commonwealth, where many wear a red poppy to recall flowers of
the fields of Flanders where thousands died in World War I. In the United States
November 11th is Veterans Day, when veterans living and dead are honored.

In 2008, on a beautiful autumn afternoon in New York City, walking down
Fifth Avenue from Fifty-Third Street following the route of the Veterans Day
parade, I stopped at Twenty-Ninth Street, where there was a flyer about the
parade tied to a fence. A group of veterans of the Korean War passed, led by
several holding a banner that read "US Marines: San Inchon, Sept 15, 1950." In
front of the Korean veterans and to their rear as well were marching bands from
distant places. One was from Bridgeport, Ohio.

The old soldiers marching that day were a reminder of the many British army
veterans of World War II who stood at attention years before on a dusty football
field to celebrate a Cameroon national day in February 1966. All of them stood
proudly, in an assortment of uniforms, caps, and medals. Older men who in their
youth might have been combatants with the 14th Army against the Japanese in
Burma or guarding prisoners of war in North Africa and the Middle East.

Years later, on 11 November 1999, there was a simple dignified ceremony in
the Bota Gardens of Cameroon on Remembrance Day. At least twenty graves of
veterans are maintained in the Botanical Garden Cemetery in the town of
Limbe. Before independence Limbe was known as Victoria.

February 1966: Njinikom Catholic Mission field: old soldiers at attention.
Photograph: Robert O'Neil

British ex-servicemen, some with campaign medals awarded for their service, mixed with veterans of the Cameroon Armed Forces. The Anglican Bishop of Douala led a prayer, wreaths were laid, and tributes given. Afterwards there was a reception at the Ex-Servicemen's Club in Limbe. It was there that some of the ex-servicemen shared briefly details of their service. A chapter in this book is devoted to that day and what they said.

Some believe that, as long as the name of a dead person is called, they remain alive to us. In this book the names of those are called who told their stories to the author.

One of the ex-soldiers who shared his story was Mr. Joseph Tepe Ndikum (see photo on p. xiii). In 1997 he visited the United States, more than fifty years after he was a soldier in the British army. His Discharge Certificate shows that he was in the 4th Battalion of the Nigeria Regiment and had served with "Colours" for 4 years and 275 days.

Off Fifth Avenue in New York City, in Madison Square Park, there is a monument called the Eternal Light Flagstaff. On the south face of the monument is the following inscription: "Erected to Commemorate the First Homecoming of the Victorious Army and Navy of These United States Officially Received by the City of New York on This Site Anno Domini MCMXVIII." Around the base of the memorial are written the names of places where great battles had been fought in France during World War I: Oise-Aisne, St. Mihiel, Cambrai, Aisne-Marne, Vittorio-Veneto, Meuse-Argonne, Somme Offensive, Champagne-Marne, Montdidier-Noyon.

Mr. J. T. Ndikum, from the bottom, third row, fifth soldier from the right. His unit was in the 4th Battalion, Nigeria Regiment. From his daughter, Mrs. Brigitte Nyada

Place-names of World War II are spoken again by old veterans in these pages. The names of some of those long-gone young men are also mentioned. Perhaps this book can be a memorial of remembrance to all who went off to war from the British Cameroons those many years ago.

This book is about them. Their testimony is at the heart of this story. It is very personal. It is not to answer all questions today about why these young men were serving Britain, the colonial power, in a war they knew little or nothing about. Nor is it to deny the darkness they witnessed but not speak of. The war for them was "No Small Thing."

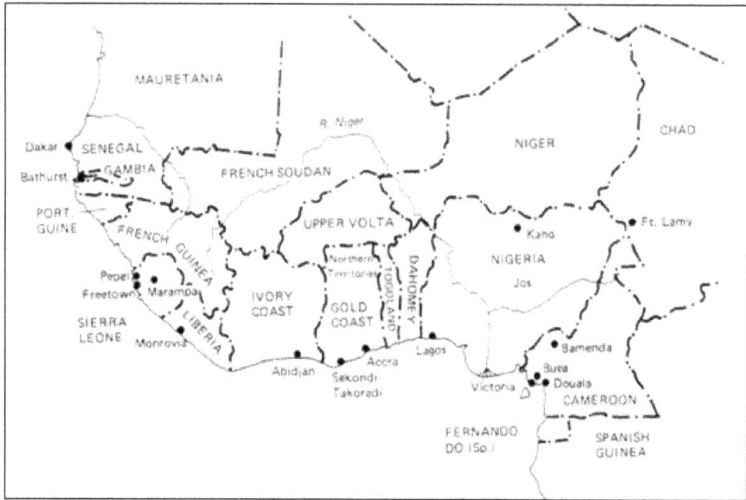

Map of West Africa: Anthony Ndi

Introduction

There are several books and articles that support the story of these soldiers in World War II. One is titled *Another Man's War*, by Barnaby Phillips.[1] It is the story of a Nigerian who was sent to Burma as part of the 81st Division, the same division in which British Cameroonians served. His story about the 81st Division going to war is theirs as well. Another is *War Bush*, by John A. L. Hamilton.[2] Hamilton was an officer in the 81st West African Division. He not only gives details about the Division but about the history of the British presence in West Africa and the formation of the Royal West African Frontier Force (RWAFF). These men were members of the RWAFF.

The first chapter of *No Small Thing* gives a brief description of the Southern British Cameroons from the end of World War I until 1939, and World War II. It aims to show where the men of this story came from and life in the British Cameroons prior to World War II.

One author in particular describes in great detail life in the country prior to the War and on to 1950. Anthony Ndi published his study in 1986 in a book titled *Africa and the Second World War*.[3]

David Killingray's book about Africa and World War II is quoted throughout this story. It is titled *Fighting for Britain, African Soldiers in the Second World War*. One reviewer wrote: "Killingray succeeds in putting human faces on some of the nearly one million African soldiers who labored and fought."

No Small Thing seeks to be a contribution to the history of a small part of Africa. It follows the defeat of Germany in her colony Kamerun by British, French, and Belgium forces during World War I. It carries on through World War II. The aim is to allow otherwise anonymous Cameroonians to speak about their own lives and their experience in the British army during World War II. And so the focus is their testimony—some in the army as combatants and others as noncombatants in garrison and support service, in West Africa, North Africa, India, and Burma.

CHAPTER 1

British Cameroons: 1916–1939

During the Summer of 1919 Britain agreed to place under the League of Nations mandates system the parts of the Cameroons she had acquired as a result of the First World War.[1]
— David E. Gardinier in *The British in Cameroons, 1919–1939.*

The following account is a belated attempt to do justice to the efforts and sacrifices of the 23,000 West Africans who as volunteers fought for King George VI in the ranks of 81 (West African) Division in Burma to explain why their campaigning there has gone almost totally unacknowledged.[2]
— John A. L. Hamilton about his book *War Bush*

We die the first time when breath leaves us. But we only truly die sometime in the future when no one speaks our name or tells our story.[3]
— R. Reese, Department of Veterans Affairs, 2021

The British Cameroons no longer exists. Her place in West African history came to an end with independence in 1961. The men interviewed in this book grew up when it was administered from Nigeria and a recruiting ground for Great Britain's Royal West African Frontier Force (RWAFF). Many served in World War II as part of the Nigeria Regiment while others were sent to North Africa. To understand who these men were and where they came from and how they became part of the British army in World War II, we go back to the years after World War I.

Judith A. Byfield, in the preface of *Africa and World War II*, writes of a concern of historians of Africa, especially those who study the Second World War. It is that inadequate attention has been given to Sub-Saharan Africa in the "major works." "For men and women across the continent, the war was not just a distant event; rather it transformed their lives, made them agents in the global struggle for democracy, and left an indelible imprint on their history"[4]

1

Almost all of those remembered in this book are from a small area of western Sub-Saharan Africa. In the late nineteenth and early twentieth century it was a German colony known as Kamerun. During World War I, Kamerun was lost to the forces of Britain, France, and Belgium in early 1916. German troops and their supporters escaped across the border into neutral Spanish Muni. With the defeat of Germany, Kamerun was divided between Britain and France, with the British area administered as part of Nigeria as a territory under the League of Nations. It came to be known as the British Cameroons.

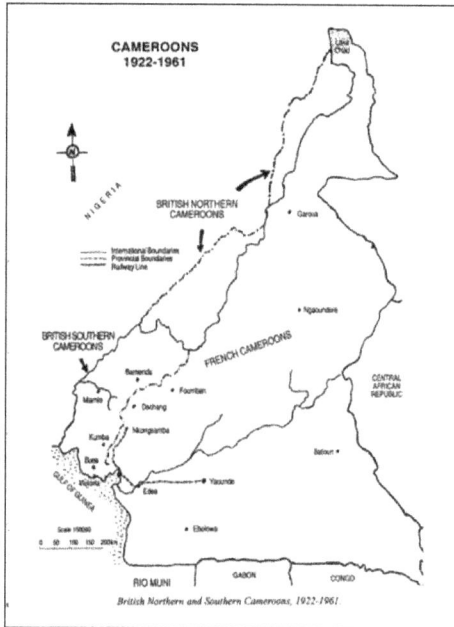

German Kamerun Divided:
A. Ndi, *Mill Hill Missionaries*, p. 15

By early 1916, at the end of the fighting in Kamerun between Germany and the Allies, the British and the French agreed to temporarily divide the German territory into what became known as the *Condominium*.

At the 11th hour on the 11th day of the 11th month of 1918, the fighting ended in Europe. The war was officially over with the signing of the Treaty of Versailles on 28 June 1919.

The decision to divide Kamerun was made in Europe. Cameroonian historian Victor Julius Ngoh reminds us that "the indigenous people were never consulted," and they never knew what had happened in Europe at Versailles. By the treaty, Germany surrendered all of her colonies in Africa including Kamerun.

At a meeting of the Allies at Versailles after the war, President Woodrow Wilson of the United States proposed a vision of a defeated Germany no longer in a place of mastery but nonetheless to be accepted as an equal among nations. In his proposal, number 5 of his Fourteen Points concerned the German colonies. He did not use the word "self-determination" but proposed "a free, open minded, and absolutely impartial adjustment of all colonial claims based upon a strict observance of the principle that in determining all such questions of sovereignty the interests of the populations concerned must have equal weight with the equitable claims of the government whose title is to be determined."[5]

Mandate

Under the League of Nations there were three types of "Mandate" for admistration of former colonies. A Class A Mandate referred to the holdings of the Ottoman Empire that were recognized as independent nations while their administration was shared between Britain and France until they were able to stand alone. Class C Mandates were the German colonies of Southwest Africa and the Pacific. Class B Mandates were the former German territories of Sub-Saharan West and Central Africa. They were judged to require a greater level of control by Britain or France, the mandatory powers, under League of Nations supervision. Under a Class B Mandate the territories were forbidden to construct military or naval bases within the mandate. Kamerun was a Class B Mandate.

The British Cameroons mandate contained two adjacent territories, Northern and Southern Cameroons. They were administered from neighboring Nigeria through a British Resident at Buea, the former German center of administration.[6] The mandate declaration of 20 July 1922 officially ended any uncertainty about the provisional British administration of the Southern Cameroons. Following the delimitation of boundaries between the French and British on 10 July 1919, the two parties worked out a set of recommendations calling on the League of Nations to approve their terms as Class B Mandates. The recommendations were sent on 17 December 1920. In the meantime, the Resident, Upton Fitzherbert Ruxton, had set in motion reforms aimed at a period of reconstruction and the establishment of the colonial order that would follow the mandate's approval. The goal was to have a period of Indirect Rule with the introduction of the Nigerian legal system and long-term administration.

British administration established colonial rule between 1923 and 1926. Resident Ruxton understood that he was to provide for the welfare of the local population and begin economic development. In order to promote local welfare, he decided it was necessary for the people to develop their own political framework to enable them to share in colonial administration. In order to build up the economy it was necessary to provide security, good roads, and taxation.

Following the conclusion of the Mandate Agreement at Geneva in mid-July of 1922, the British proceeded, through the Order of Council of 26 June 1923, to make permanent the temporary arrangement under which Bamenda and three other divisions of the Southern Cameroons territory were administered from Southern Nigeria.[7]

Plantations

Revitalizing the economy meant that the plantations of the German Kamerun needed to be working at full capacity again. Many of the men recruited for the army during World War II were workers on those plantations near the coast or were employed in places associated with the plantations.

When the British army took control of the Kumba and Victoria area during World War I, they interned the German technicians and plantation managers. When the fighting in Kamerun ended in 1916, the plantations were merged and a department of the Nigerian government was formed to maintain them until they could be disposed of after the war. The British recognized the land sales made by the German government with the local people, rejecting as impracticable the idea that plantations be returned to their earlier tribal owners. And so in 1923 they looked for non-German buyers for the plantation estates. The British rejected the bids of a first auction. In 1924 they allowed the original German owners, aided by the German government in another auction, to repurchase their former plantations.

The former German owners knew the value of their former property and wanted their plantations back. For example, the Moliwe Estate was made up of 32,067 acres with sixty buildings and a section of furnished housing. There was also a hospital.

During the interwar period, workers began to immigrate from the Cameroon Grassfields and Nigeria on a large scale to work on the plantations. The local population could not supply the labor needed on the estates. In 1927, 10,542 plantation workers were living in Victoria Division, yet only 722 were locals.[8]

Within two years the German managers and technicians had the plantations operating at prewar capacity and were expanding. They enlarged the ports at Tiko and Victoria. In 1927, the plantations employed 13,000 Africans, and in 1935, 15,691.[9]

By 1938, Germans were the largest group of Europeans in the British Cameroons. There were three times as many Germans as there were British nationals. "When Hitler began the Austrian *Anschluss* in March 1938 there were celebrations in Victoria Division, and the Nazi flag was even hoisted in Victoria. Between 1925 and 1939, most of the trade between British Cameroon and Europe was with Germany."[10] When World War II began, German property was again expropriated by the Custodian of Enemy Property. With this act German activity came to an end.

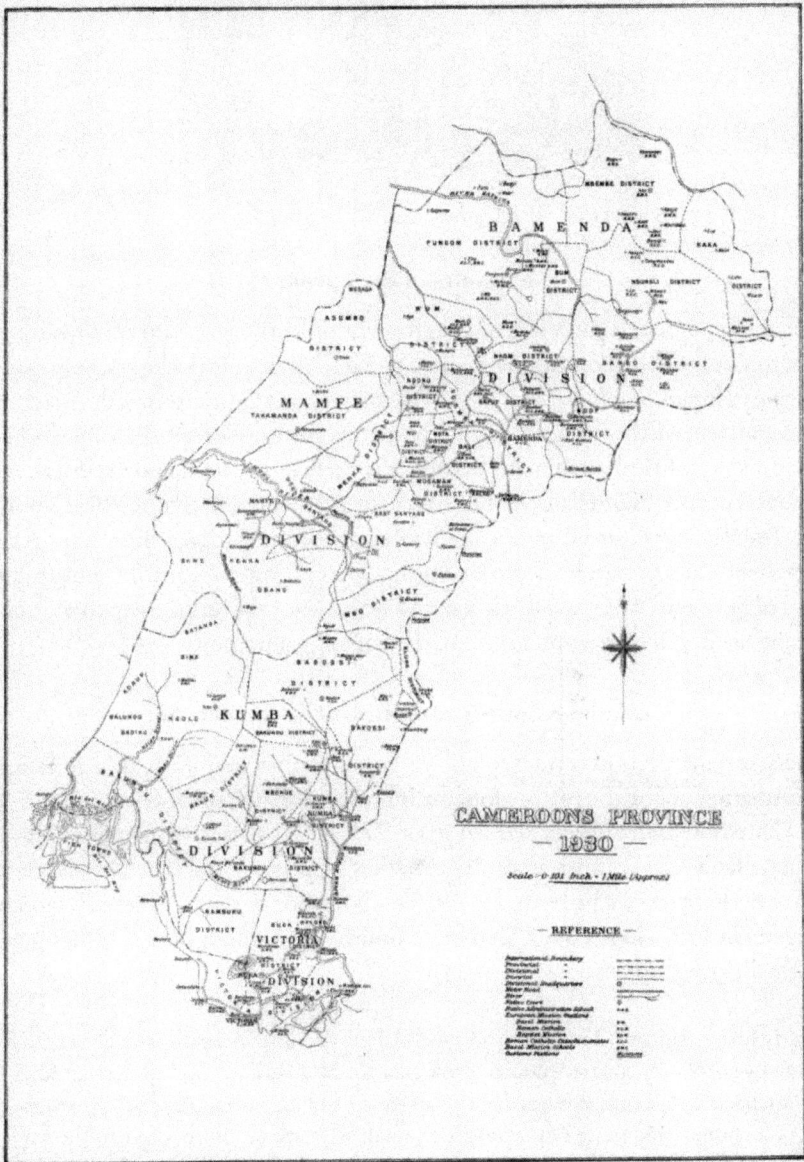

Cameroons Province 1930. Source: Buea Archive

Flag of British Cameroons. WikiCommons

Memoirs of Europeans

Official reports and memoirs of government officers can be a useful source of information about conditions in British West Africa, including Cameroons, during colonial times. Dr. Emeka Anyaoku, who was Commonweath Secretary General, was of the opinion that colonial memoirs are of special value as historical and political documents because they reflect the firsthand experience of colonial officers. For example, Dr. Anyaoku considered Malcom Milne's book *No Telephone to Heaven*, an outsider's tale of the local peoples' most important experience at the hands of the colonizer, to be "a timely contribution to our shared heritage."[11] Milne's work was one story. Another was the experience of a young Sir Bryan Sharwood Smith in the British Cameroons.

Colonial Administrator in British Cameroons

The assessment reports and book of Sir Bryan Sharwood Smith are a source of information about the early colonial administration of British Cameroons.[12]

Sharwood Smith's book *But Always as Friends* is a narrative of his 37 years of experience as an administrative officer in the Cameroons and Northern Nigeria. After his long service he retired in 1957 as Governor of the Northern Region of Nigeria in 1957. In his book Sharwood Smith writes about his first assignment in the British Cameroons:

> My first Resident, "Tin Eye" Anderson, a dour and uncommunicative Scot with an eyeglass, was succeeded after a few months by Major U. F. H. Ruxton, a shy intellectual and one of Lugard's original band of soldier administrators. Ruxton's quiet humor and sense of purpose soon made its mark on those who had the wit to understand and follow his lead. But with the idle and pretentious it was another matter.

Ruxton, as we have seen already, was Senior Resident of the British Cameroons under the League of Nations mandate from 1921 to 1925. The British mandate was for two adjacent territories, Northern and Southern Cameroons. The headquarters for the administration was at Buea in Southern Cameroons.

Sir Bryan Evers Sharwood Smith.
By Walter Stoneman.
Permission: National Portrait Gallery

Major Upton Fitzherbert Ruxton was born 8 November 1873, the son of an admiral in the British navy. In World War I, he served as a captain in the Worchester Regiment and later in the Nigeria Regiment. Ruxton's sister Sylvia married a Canadian officer, Arthur Leith-Ross, who served with Ruxton in Northern Nigeria. He died of blackwater fever in 1908. His widow, Ruxton's sister, remained in Nigeria and became a well-known writer and anthropologist. In 1925, Major Ruxton became Lt. Governor of the Southern Provinces of Nigeria. It is he who wrote the report on the administration of the mandate for the British Cameroons in 1924 for the League of Nations. Major Ruxton died in London in 1954.

Again Sharwood Smith:[13]

Language of the Southern Cameroons
The lingua franca of the Southern Cameroons was pidgin English. . . . Built over a century or more round a hard core of English, it conforms to a definite pattern of grammar and syntax. It is, furthermore, highly tonal and extremely expressive. . . . I tried to speak it accurately and with the correct intonation, for it was the only means of communication short of using an interpreter.

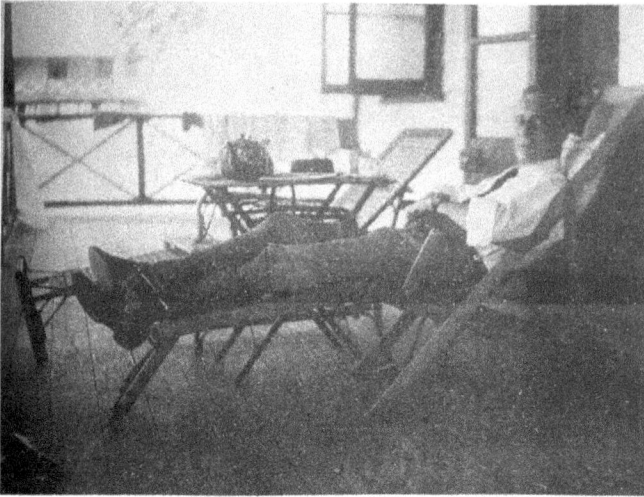

Upton Fitzherbert Ruxton, in "Silent Heritage: Investigating Ruxton's Nigeria Collection at the Hornimam Museum and Gardens," *Itinerario* 47 (2023): 257–77, 262. The photo first appeared in Sylvia Leith-Ross, *Stepping Stones: Memoirs of Colonial Nigeria, 1907–1960* (London: Peter Owen, [1960] 1983).
Source: Creative Commons

Travel to Bamenda, 1924
Bamenda was sixteen days' trek from the coast, and on the fourteenth day, as I breasted the escarpment, a little breathless from the three-thousand-foot climb, I sniffed the cool hill air with appreciation. No more fetid forests, no more sullen forest dwellers, ridden with superstition. In their place, a cooler, fresher world. Here were rolling grasslands amid which, in tall grass-thatched huts, lived a more virile and a more friendly people, ready with their laughter and ready with a greeting to the passing stranger.

The departure of the troops from Bamenda was, before long, to cause trouble. They had been withdrawn . . . because(the) League of Nations . . . felt that a military garrison in mandated territory was inappropriate, especially as the Bamenda people, who made very good soldiers, were enlisting in the Nigerian Regiment in considerable numbers.

Employment

Greater mobility had already been experienced by large numbers of the male population, beginning with the bands of labor recruits introduced to the economic and administrative centers of German colonialism. It was in 1925 that the real revitalization of the coastal plantations began and once again attracted thousands of Grassfielders.[14]

Seal of the British Cameroons.
Source: WikiCommons

The colonial system increased mobility that went hand in hand with trading ventures, plantation labor, and employment on the Mamfe-Bamenda Road project, along with other evidence of economic change. The reconstruction of German paths and the tracing of Native Authority roads were underway after World War I. The first survey for the Mamfe-Bamenda Road was undertaken in 1923.[15]

Education

Government policy in the British Cameroons was formed by following the findings of the Phelps-Stokes Report of 1919. This report was the first to study African education in the hands of mission agencies. The report emphasized that the African way of life was dignified and could not be assessed in Western terms. Furthermore, it stated that

> with full appreciation of the heroic service rendered by missionaries to Africa, it must be urged that those who disregard the values of organization and supervision are neglecting two of the elements most essential to the success of their efforts. While this neglect may be overlooked in the pioneer work of early missionaries, it should not be tolerated in this day when even casual observation of mission work in any part of the world shows clearly the wastefulness of non-organized and unsupervised activities in home and foreign missions.[16]

On 24 November 1923, a committee was established to advise the Secretary of State for Colonies on "native" education. In 1925, a memorandum on education stressed the need to upgrade village education, provide a system of visiting teachers, provide grants-in-aid to missions who met standards, set up advisory boards, and require education authorities to adapt to local conditions. Cameroons was then administered under the Nigerian Educational Ordinances as a rural area of Eastern Nigeria. The ordinances were amended by E. R. J. Hussey, Director of Education, in 1928, and again in 1931, when he observed that education had been considered by some in colonial administration to be "a menace," and that the voluntary agencies were often not seen in terms of political development but, on the contrary, as instruments to achieve docility and obedience to the administration. It was some time before it was realized that what was needed was not less education but more.

Roman Catholic Missions

German Catholic missionaries were forced to abandon their work during World War I. The story of the Catholic Mission in the British mandate between wars is very much the story of the London-based Mill Hill Missionaries and their Cameroonian coworkers.

The first four missionaries from Mill Hill in London arrived in Cameroon at Victoria on Sunday, 26 March 1922. The next day they met a catechist and a group of Christians. The catechists had been trained and carried on in the absence of the German missionaries. Resident Ruxton told the missionaries that there was a great cry for them all over the province. By the end of 1923 the mission reported that there were 7,363 Catholics, 4,512 school children, 7 priests, 165 catechists, and 15 schoolteachers in the prefecture of Buea.[17]

Under E. R. J. Hussey many recommendations were made that improved the standard of education in Cameroons, and, under Bishop Peter Rogan, the Catholic mission continued to build an educational infrastructure even when government resources were inadequate.

By 1935, the foundations of a Catholic primary school system had been laid at Shisong, Sasse, Bonjongo, Baseng, and Njinikom. Soon every new mission became closely connected with a primary school. At a time when there were few or no subsidies, the mission had over a hundred schools.

When World War II began in September 1939, according to the British administration, all German, Austrian, and Italian nationals in the Cameroons became potential enemy agents. The Catholic mission lost seven missionaries. They were taken into custody and transported to Nigeria and then from Lagos to Kingston, Jamaica, where they landed on 3 December 1940. They remained interned on Jamaica until 1946.[18]

Fr. Thomas Mulligan, a Mill Hill Missionary, wrote about the war years in the early 1970s. He reflected on the internment of missionaries.

> "In September 1939 World War Two broke out. This had an almost immediate impact on Southern Cameroons for since 1925 very many of the Germans who had owned and worked the plantations returned to take over again. These Ger-

man nationals, along with German and Italian missionaries, were labelled 'enemy aliens' and as such were interned either in Umahia or in Jamaica. Practically all the reverend sisters in Shisong were Tyrolese and were reckoned to be Italians because they carried Italian passports. However, the wonderful work that they were doing endeared them even to the British and Allied government so that the stigma of 'enemy' was taken from them and they were allowed to stay and get on with their charitable missionary work in child-welfare, health-care, education and domestic science. In this darkest hour for the missions, the Mill Hill missionaries, whose members were mainly British, Irish or Dutch nationality, found themselves a source of stability during the war and in the post-war period, providing education at primary, secondary and teacher-training levels."[19]

Bishop Peter Rogan and Fr. Aloysius Wankuy, first Roman Catholic priest from British Cameroons, Shisong, 1949. Mill Hill Archives Freshfield, UK

Baptist Missions

The work of the Baptist mission continued but struggled after World War I. One missionary, Jakob Bender, wrote that, since the war, Mr. Laban Mok, an ordained Cameroonian, was in charge, and the number of his stations numbered fourteen. Unfortunately "most of the teachers were insufficiently trained and the funds inadequate to keep them." Nevertheless Baptist work expanded during the 1920s. Men who had come to the coast from the Grassfields to work in the plantations were evangelized by the German Baptists. They then returned home to establish local churches. The situation changed in 1927, when the German Mission Ordinance was repealed by the Nigerian government and property confiscated during the war was returned to former German missionary societies. German Baptist missionaries began to return in January 1927.

The main Baptist school in the interwar period was at Soppo. It was established in 1927, and by 1940 it was the largest in British Cameroons. The school was meant to support the church workers, evangelists, and teachers and to provide a steady stream of Africans to promote the church. The initiative and leadership among African Baptists really shaped the growth of Baptist churches and schools as well as the life of many people under colonial rule. Years later, one missionary estimated that a large percentage of Baptist school graduates completed their studies and then they went on to be employed in many occupations: mechanics, independent shop owners, government workers, teachers, church workers, and clerks and commercial workers.[20]

Carl Jacob Bender was a German Baptist missionary pioneer in Cameroon first in Douala and later in Soppo. Because he was a citizen of the United States he was allowed to remain during the war years only leaving in 1919. He spent the next years in the United States, serving churches and publishing ethnological books, but when missionaries were permitted to return, he was recalled to his old station at Soppo in 1929. He revived the dormant work and built a new church building before dying from blackwater fever in 1935.[21]

Basel Mission

During World War I all the schools started by German missionaries and the government were closed. Vernacular schools, those that taught in a local language, reopened after some time, and so when the missionaries returned in 1925 the only areas that were without village schools were Buea and Besonabang. The education department considered the vernacular school to be substandard. Yet at the end of 1925 the Basel Mission had 114 vernacular schools with 3,207 children. Two years later there were 299 vernacular schools with 7,155 boys and girls. In 1926 the Lagos government considered closing the Basel Mission vernacular schools. Thanks to Resident Ruxton, the Basel Mission was allowed to register the vernacular schools as religious schools in which reading, writing, and religious instructions in the local language were allowed.

The first three primary schools were opened in 1929 and staffed with Europeans. They were at Bali, Besonabang, and Buea. The language of instruction was either in the Bali or Douala language. In 1931 a fourth school was opened at Nyasoso. Beginning in 1932, the mission primary schools received government grants, but they had classes only to Standard 4.

At the beginning of World War II, the Basel Mission was running 15 primary schools. By 1940 there were 1,262 children in the primary schools. In the vernacular/religious schools there were 5,030 children. There was always a shortage of trained teachers. In 1941 out of 58 primary school teachers only 12 were elementary trained.[22]

Anthony Ndi has written about the impact of the Christian missions during the period between the wars. The influence of the Roman Catholic, Baptist, and Basel missions grew because they were "essentially [a] grassroots, heart-to-heart phenomenon" that penetrated "right into the interior of the country."[23]

Political Life in the British Cameroons

Victor T. LeVine has written about this period prior to World War II in his book *The Cameroons: From Mandate to Independence.* The presence of many Germans in the British Cameroons and the rise of the Nazi movement among them alarmed the administration before the war. The repurchase of nearly all their former property by German owners in 1924 meant that more than 207,000 acres were returned to them, and, by the eve of the Second World War in 1938, it was slightly more. The sales brought Germans back to Cameroon "with a vengeance." By 1938 there were a total of 285 Germans in British Cameroons to 86 British. "During the middle and late 1930s Germany intensified her propaganda campaign for recovery of her colonies." Reports circulated that many African Cameroonians "ardently wished a return of the German administration." On 13 March 1938 Nazi Germany incorporated Austria into the "Reich." The Austrian annexation was called the *Anschluss.*

In the British Cameroons, the *Anschluss* was celebrated by the sizable group of Germans in the Victoria area. A German propaganda publication of the time includes pictures of a light railway train in a banana plantation carrying German settlers and emblazoned with banners reading "Der Führer in Kamerun"; the hoisting of a Nazi flag at Victoria; and the visit of an official ship to Tiko.

Agitation in Cameroon was a reflection of the efforts of the Weimar and Nazi governments to regain the old German colonies. Under the Nazis this was especially felt in the mandates.

"The Camerouns floundered (as did the other French and British mandates) in a sea of French and British attempts at colonial appeasement. . . . It was the Cameroon's good fortune that both France and Britain did not come to terms with Hitler on this question of claims on former German territory."

"The mandate period really ended in 1940 with World War II. The League of Nations collapsed and with it the mandates. The only question that seemed important "was whether the mandates could be kept out of German hands."

"In the case of the Cameroons, the picture became blurred because of the presence of the nominal government in Vichy after 1940. That Vichy failed to maintain the loyalty of the Cameroons is probably attributable to the vigor of the local (colonial) administration, which, although it did not like Philippe Pétain and the Vichy government, liked the prospects of a return of German rule even less."

The collapse of France in June 1940 left French Cameroun without direction. But by the end of June most French territories swore allegiance to Marshall Pétain's Vichy government. The majority of French settlers and African elites realized that this might mean incorporation into Hitler's Greater Germany (*Grossdeutschland*). Again this was a result of propaganda about the return of the African mandates to Germany. But, by late August, the Vichy administration was upset. During the night of 26 August and the next morning, Colonel Philippe Leclerc, an emissary of the Free French and General Charles de Gaulle, traveled by canoe from Tiko in the British mandate to Douala with twenty-four companions. They were met by partisans, and soon the French mandate was in the hands of the Free French. De Gaulle sent a cable to the League of Nations Secretariat that, as leader of the Free French, he had taken over administration of the mandate.[24]

General Charles de Gaulle, 1942.
Source: WikiCommons

The British Cameroons at the time of World War II had an estimated population of 400,000. From this number about 3,500 enlisted in the British army[25]—not large numbers but an important contribution to the forces raised in Nigeria

CHAPTER 2

World War II and the Royal West African Frontier Force

The West African Frontier Force, granted the prefix "Royal" in 1928, known for short as the "WAFF" (pronounced Woff), whose European members were proud to be known as "Waffs," existed under that name from 1898 to 1960 as the armed forces of the four former West African colonies of Great Britain.
—Hamilton, *War Bush*, 23

Until the early 1930s, the British Army in Africa, excluding white-run South Africa, had numbered a paltry 15,000 men. By the end of the war in 1945, some 500,000 Africans had worn the British uniform.
—Phillips, *Another Man's War*, 20

World War Two Begins

In 1939 the British Empire included Crown Colonies, Protectorates, and India. There were also ties to the Dominions of Australia, Canada, South Africa, and New Zealand. In West Africa, Sierra Leone, Gambia, Gold Coast (Ghana), and Nigeria, including the Cameroons, were part of the British Empire, as was Burma in Asia. With independent Egypt there was a treaty in 1936 that allowed Britain to defend the Suez Canal.

At the outbreak of war in Europe, therefore, Britain held sixteen territories in Africa covering more than 3,600,000 square miles, with a population of about fifty million people. Her African military numbered fewer than 15,000. One priority for Britain was to protect the Suez Canal and the sea route around the Cape at South Africa.

In addition, the natural resources of Sub-Saharan Africa, especially rubber, became vital, particularly after the fall of Malaya to Japan in 1942. The Italian presence in Africa had also become a challenge to the British and the French. Fascist Italy, a nationalist, authoritarian, and anti-communist dictatorship under Benito Mussolini, was seen as the greatest threat to French and British colonies in Africa. Italy had controlled Libya since 1912 and, in 1935, invaded Abyssinia, where they were defeated. But, by 1939, Italy had colonial divisions of about 60,000, mostly troops from Eritrea and Somalia. There was also a large, well-equipped Italian army. "By 1940 the Italians claimed an army of quarter of a million *ascari* (indigenous African soldiers) in their enlarged *Africa Orientale Italiana*."[1] To meet this threat, the Kings African Rifles, the armed forces of Great Britain in East Africa, was expanded after 1938.

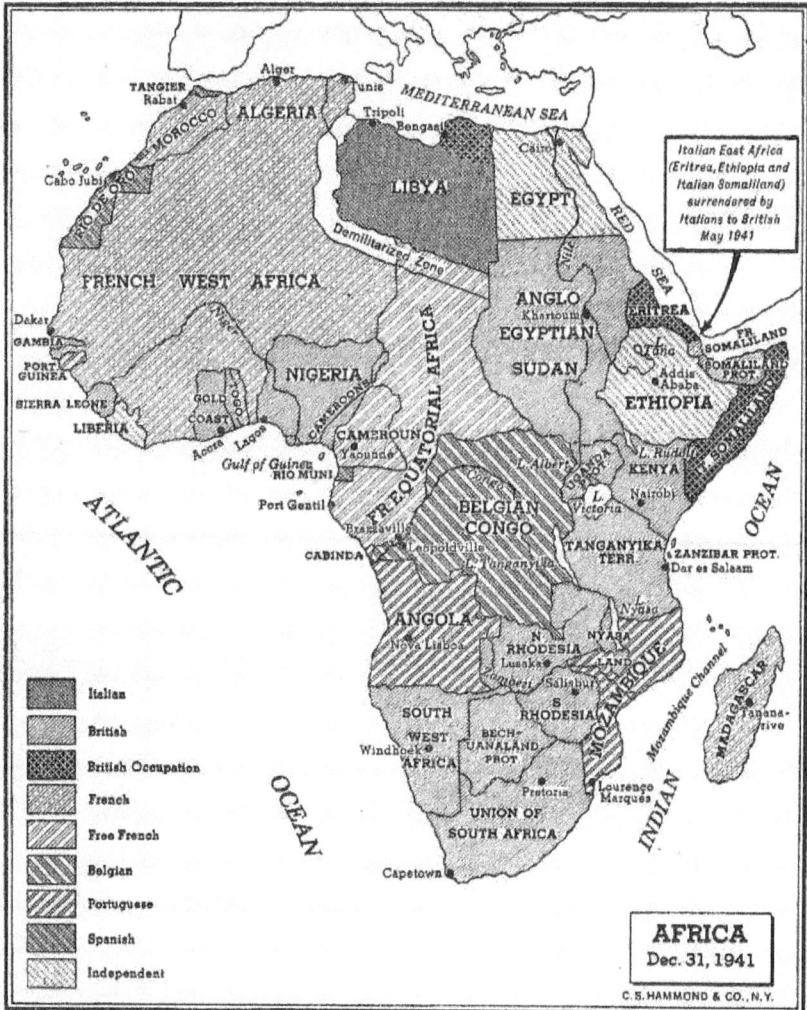

Italian East Africa (Eritrea, Ethiopia and Italian Somaliland) surrendered by Italians to British May 1941

Legend:
- Italian
- British
- British Occupation
- French
- Free French
- Belgian
- Portuguese
- Spanish
- Independent

AFRICA
Dec. 31, 1941

C.S. HAMMOND & CO., N.Y.

One of the countries in Asia that was part of the British Empire was Burma, now called Myanmar. British rule began with the three Anglo-Burmese Wars between 1824 and 1885. During World War II, in 1941, Japan invaded Burma and threatened to invade India. The Japanese occupied Burma until 1945, when a British-led invasion supported by Commonwealth armies that included

Cameroonians and with the United States drove out the Japanese. Near the end of the war, a Burma National Army also rose against the Japanese on 27 March 1945.

World War II began far away from Burma and the British Cameroons, in September 1939. Germany invaded Poland on the 1st of September, and on the 3rd Britain and France honored an agreement with Poland by declaring war on Germany.

Germany then turned west and attacked France in June 1940. At the time, France had control of territories in North Africa, West Africa, Equatorial Africa, and Madagascar. She also had 100,000 Africans soldiers under arms with 75,000 either in France or on the way to France. Some estimates put casualties at 24,000, with 15,000–16,000 captured by the Germans. When France was defeated, an armistice was signed that divided France between the Germans and a collabo-rating French government at Vichy. This meant that the pro-German Vichy government controlled French Africa and that African troops commanded by French officers were not fighting against Nazi Germany along with the Allies. A Vichy-controlled French Camerouns became a danger to Nigeria. This changed when Equatorial Africa joined the cause of the Free French under General Charles de Gaulle.

Italy entered the war on 10 June 1940, supporting Germany by attacking southern France on the 21 June. On 13 September, the Italians then invaded British-controlled Egypt from Libya. Two weeks later on 27 September, Ger-many, Italy, and Japan signed a tripartite pact.

To support Italy in North Africa, Germany sent its *Afrika* Corps in February 1941. By June 1942 German forces, supporting the Italians, entered Egypt. But in October the British defeated an army of Germans and Italians at El Alamein in Egypt driving them in retreat to the border between Libya and Tunisia. On 8 November British and United States forces landed in Algeria and Morocco. In May 1943 the German and Italian armies surrendered to the Allies, and the War in North Africa came to an end. Control of and guarding of the prisoners of war became the duty of troops from West Africa including Cameroonians. "British West African units went to North Africa and Palestine as garrison troops and guards for POWs."[2]

In the Pacific on 7 December, Japan bombed Pearl Harbor, and the United States declared war. On 8 December, Japan invaded the Philippines, French Indo-China, and British Singapore. By May 1942 Japan was in control of Burma and was threatening India.

"The course of the war in Europe, the role of African troops in defeating the Italians in East Africa, the military and labour demands placed on Africa for the North African campaign, and the Japanese threat to India in 1942–43 deter-mined that African soldiers would play a much more prominent role overseas than was demanded of them in the Great War of 1914–1918."[3]

The Royal West African Frontier Force

A badge of the Royal West African
Frontier Force (RWAFF)

The British army in West Africa was called the *Royal West African Frontier Force*.
It was made up of men from Nigeria, Gold Coast (Ghana), Sierra Leone, and
Gambia. The largest number came from Nigeria and included the British Cameroons. The force originated in the armed police that had been set up to maintain law and order. These constabularies in Lagos, Niger, and Niger Coast were
joined together in 1899 to form the Nigeria Regiment. This regiment fought in
the Second Ashanti War in 1900. In 1901 the West African Frontier Force was
raised. In 1914 the two Nigerian Regiments were joined and fought against the
Germans in Kamerun and East Africa. After World War I, in 1928, the WAFF
became the Royal West African Frontier Force (RWAFF). It was led by British
officers, and all the other West African ranks were directed by British Warrant
Officers (WOs) and Non-Commissioned Officers (NCOs). About five hundred Europeans from Rhodesia went to Nigeria in 1939 to serve with the
RWAFF. Many of them fought in Burma and many of these officers, WOs and
NCOs, remained with them until the end of the war.

At the beginning of World War II, Nigeria had three full-strength battalions and two others at half-strength. Gold Coast had one and a half battalions.
Sierra Leone had one battalion and The Gambia had one company. Nigeria
would increase from five battalions to thirteen; Gold Coast to nine battalions;
Sierra Leone to two battalions, and The Gambia to two battalions.

In May 1940, two brigades from Gold Coast and Nigeria sailed for East
Africa, arriving at Mombasa at the end of June. Gold Coast joined the 12th
African Division and the Nigerians joined the 11th Division. The Nigerian
Brigade was part of the spearhead on Mogadishu and Harare against Italy. The
West African Brigades were withdrawn in September 1941 and returned to

West Africa. They were to help to organize the 81st and 82nd West African Divisions that went to the war in Burma against the Japanese.

At the same time, the expansion of the Royal West African Frontier Force continued. When France fell to Germany in 1940, mounted infantry units and a reconnaissance regiment were formed to control the borders. By the end of 1941, Nigeria had raised thirteen battalions of infantry and other units.

Forty-three pioneer (work) battalions were formed and also a second group of twenty garrison (guard duty) troops into five companies. They saw service in the Middle East, Palestine, Morocco, and Sicily. This was where many from British Cameroons were sent.

By 1944, the RWAFF had two complete divisions in the field. The 81st (West African) Division was formed on 1 March 1943 and arrived in India at the end of the year. The 82nd (West African) Division was formed in August 1943 and arrived in India in the summer of 1944. In November 1943, the 3rd WA Brigade, consisting of the 6th, 7th and 12th Nigeria Regiments was ordered to serve under General Orde Wingate with his Long Range Penetration Group.[4]

Men from the British Cameroons were part of the Nigerian troops assigned to work and garrison duty in North Africa and to the 81st and 82nd Divisions that were put together to join the fight in Burma.

CHAPTER 3

Recruitment

During the War years several hundred thousand men were recruited for military service, most enlisting voluntarily but some as a result of varying degrees of pressure, including force.

—Killingray, *Fighting for Britain*, 37

Indeed, Cameroon was a League of Nations mandate and conscription was forbidden there.

—Echenberg, *Colonial Conscripts*, 75

One recruit, asked if he agreed to sign up for the "duration of the war" asked "What war?"

—Bull, *Palm Oil Chop*, 69[1]

Background

Barnaby Phillips, in his book *Another Man's War,* describes how one young man was recruited in southwestern Nigeria to join the Royal West African Frontier Force.[2]

So it was on this December day that the smartly dressed man took up his position by the Olowo's palace, and began his speech. He was talking about what Hitler might do to Africans, but that wasn't all. He was urging the men who'd gathered round him to sign up and fight. Not just for Owo, but for Nigeria, the British Empire and King George. At that, someone in the crowd cheered, and Isaac's curiosity got the better of him.

He was barely sixteen, but he was an imposing boy, already almost six feet tall, and he knew his own mind. He pushed his way through, closer to the lorry, so he could better hear what the recruiting officer was saying. Nigerians faced a stark choice, said the officer: to live under British justice, "the finest system in the world" he called it, or to be slaves under Hitler. It was a hot day, and the officer knew he would not have his audience's attention for long if he only stuck to rhetoric. People needed to hear practicalities. Join up, he said, because the pay is good, the uniforms are dashing, and, when the war is over, you will be the first in line for all the good jobs, maybe even in government service. The officer kept his message simple, as he'd been told to do, and he was rewarded with murmurs of approval. He was sure of one thing: he had no time to sit in the village of Emure-Ile and rot his life away. He began looking for ways to escape. The army propaganda team rolled into Owo a few days after Isaac received the disappointing news about his exams. Standing in the palace of the Olowo, he had listened intently to what the recruiting officer had to say.... The following morning... Isaac set out... on a lorry... all the way to the town of Abeokuta. There he signed up with the Royal West African Frontier Force, swearing an oath of loyalty to King and Empire with a Bible pressed to his forehead. He had become a British soldier.

There was another swearing in oath for African followers of traditional religions, taken while kissing a bayonet: "If I am disloyal or shown fear in battle, let this bayonet drink my blood."[3]

As early as February 1939 the Secretary of State at Enugu in Nigeria sent instructions to the administration in British Cameroons giving the minimum requirements for those applying to join the army. An applicant must be at least 5 feet 4 inches in height, have an unexpanded chest measurement of 34 inches and have sound heart and lungs. He added that the "applicant" must be a laborer, an agriculturist, or a hunter, etc.[4]

There has been a question whether African soldiers were volunteers or were conscripted. The *New York Times* ran a story on 1 April 2000 about an ex-soldier in Gambia who had fought the Japanese in Burma. Barkary Dibba was "known as the last survivor among the ten local men who had fought in the army against Japan's Imperial Army in Burma." The author Norimitsu Onishi writes of the young men who were "drafted" like Mr. Dibba "from the remotest corners of the African colonies and sent . . . to places they never knew existed." Dibba is reported to have said that British officers came for one week to his village of several hundred farmers "searching for volunteers." There was one rally where drums were played to stir up enthusiasm but there was "no volunteer." Afterwards the chief went to each compound and demanded one volunteer. "When they saw you they would just grip you and take you." The "conscripts" from Gambia, the author writes were then sent for training in Nigeria.[5]

The article was shown to John Hamilton, who wrote, "Despite frequent assertions to the contrary we had no need to conscript or forcibly enlist men." Hamilton found that the veterans of World War II "are intensely proud of their service and their medals." He added that many recruits in the Cameroons were enlisted in the Pioneer Corps, with some of these sent to the Middle East, Palestine, and North Africa. "Not surprisingly much less is known about them than the combatant units."[6]

In French Cameroun, although it was a League of Nations mandate like the British Cameroons, and therefore conscription of Africans was prohibited, authorities might not pursue men of military age traveling to Nigeria to enlist as a substitute for a local recruit. There is a "conservative estimate" that the French "recruited in excess of 200,000 black Africans during the Second World War." A conscription law of 1919 "had made military service a universal male obligation." War aims were communicated, for example, by the comic strip *"Mamadou s'en va t'en guerre."* It was stressed that Africans were expected to play a significant role "in aid of the Motherland."[7]

David Killingray estimated that, of the many thousands who were recruited for military service, most enlisted voluntarily but "some as a result of varying degrees of pressure, including force. . . . While conscription across Africa was generally avoided, it would be quite wrong to infer that all recruitment was voluntary." For the most part Britain's peacetime colonial armies were composed of mercenaries and were drawn from peripheral areas of the colony or from neighboring territories. Men sent by chiefs as possible recruits were often rejected as "medically unfit." In late 1941 a conscription ordinance was introduced in the southern Gold Coast in order "to secure motor drivers and artisans." A similar ordinance was introduced elsewhere as well. Killingray concludes that most men enlisted as volunteers but a distinction between volunteers and conscripts "is not always easy to make."[8]

Among the specialist units provided by West Africa were four Medical Units, comprising orderlies trained by the West African Army Medical Corps. They were attached to British hospitals in Sicily and Italy. South Africans were also drawn into the war. The Native Military Corps were formed in 1940. They and the "coloureds" in the South African army were not trained in the use of firearms.

Generally, it was not thought appropriate for Africans or people of African descent to kill whites, but this view did not apply to Indians. Troops from Bechuanaland, for example, were at first used as pioneer (labor) corps and for guard duty in North Africa and Syria. In 1943, however, six Bechuana companies were retrained as anti-aircraft crews and stationed first in North Africa and then in Sicily. Some, retrained for smoke-making, supported the Indian and Maori assault troops at Monte Cassino. Bechuana pioneers moved northward through Italy with the Allied troops. Of these 10,000 Bechuana troops, seventeen were killed and forty-two were "mentioned in despatches" for their bravery.[9]

In a 2020 article in the *Journal of African Military History*, Oliver Coates suggests that "we should attempt to distinguish between combatants and non-combatants." Therefore Cameroonians served in North Africa on garrison duties and guarding prisoners of war. They were mostly members of the "pioneer" corps and were noncombatants. In India and Burma they became combatants fighting the Japanese. The recruitment of soldiers and pioneers is still a controversial topic "because it shows the extent of British-instigated coercion in the conscription and involuntary recruitment of soldiers, army labourers, and clerks."[10] In interviews with veterans none made a distinction. Whatever they did, combatants in Burma or guarding POWs in North Africa, they did as British soldiers.

An issue that may have contributed to the grievances of ex-servicemen was the "wartime prestige of all those who could pass themselves off as 'soldiers.'" This has contributed to debates about war veterans or "the recurrent tendency of non-combatant military labourers to assert their identity as "soldiers." While newer themes in the study of World War II in West Africa have emerged, "core subjects such as recruitment are still of vital importance."[11]

Almost forty years ago, Cameroon Professor Anthony Ndi wrote about recruitment of British Cameroonians for the British army during World War II:

> On the whole, the prosecution of the Second World War appears never to have elicited popular support among the people of Southern Cameroon, partly as a result of resilient German propaganda, but mostly because of the nature of British administration, which had never been inspiring. This was reflected in the poor response to recruitment and in the general attitude of the people towards the war.
>
> With an estimated population of over 400,000, barely 3500 Cameroonians enlisted as soldiers. . . . The basic qualities required by the army were that recruits should reach the prescribed age and standard was that he "be a farm laborer, agriculturist or hunter; used to an outdoor life and able to march barefooted."
>
> The initial recruiting drive was met with enthusiasm but as the war progressed the numbers dropped drastically. . . .
>
> Reviewing the recruitment situation well into the middle of the war, the Resident, Mr. A. M. Muir, opposed the introduction of conscription in Cameroon, explaining that, of a gang of Cameroonians carefully recruited overnight, there was always sure to be some 10 per cent missing in the morning. . . . Cameroonians, he observed, were "loyal" devoted and hardworking people but it was pointless asking them to register to fight in a war which they were told no longer threatened their country. Mr. Muir considered it dangerous to introduce conscription in Cameroon. . . .

He also could have added that the Administration was overstretched and that the Native Authorities were wholly incompetent to enforce conscription.[12]

British Cameroonians and Recruitment

The Buea Archives had information about recruits and among them men who were serving as drivers and signalmen.

The following served as drivers in the army in 1941: Evaris Esimi from Tiko; Denis Kumenda from Bokchamini village; and Raphael Minge from Ngeme Victoria.

The following served as wireless operators: Gregory Dinge from Baligam of the Bamenda Division; John Talbot from Bessonabang (he worked as a signalman in India. He wrote to the District Officer (DO) on 21 February 1941 asking to know what is happening with his parents back in Cameroon; Jonas

Tabe Agbo, of 4th Battalion of the Nigerian Regiment, Royal West African Frontier Force, wrote to the DO in Mamfe on the 2 September 1942 asking him to forward 6 pounds 10 shillings to his sister, Madam Hana Maliba of Batoke in Victoria; Martin Abunaw, who served as a signalman, wrote on 9 December 1943 complaining that there were only two of them serving at the station; and Ndan Nwanake in a letter written by his father Bawe Tiku asking his whereabouts. It had been three years since he had heard from him.[13]

These were among the men recruited for their skills as drivers, or "artisans" in the official directives from the Buea Archive, while many more were needed for the Pioneers and support services.

Those with a Skill

Joseph Tepe Ndikum of Bamenda and **Njei Moses Timah** were drivers on the rough unpaved road between Mamfe and Bamenda. From Mamfe there was a road to Eastern Nigeria and another to the southwest to Kumba and on to Victoria and Douala.

Joseph was stopped near the market at Guzang in Moghamo. He said that soldiers ordered him out of his motor, a truck, and into their motor and on to the Bamenda station. He slept at Bamenda for a night and then went down to Victoria where he "shaved and was thrown all the army clothes."

Mr. J. T. Ndikum with his lorry in 1960s Bamenda.
Photo: R. O'Neil

Moses was a driver on the same road but carried passengers from Douala on the coast. He was driving to Bamenda and was stopped at Bali by "white soldiers." He said he was forced to abandon the vehicle with its passengers. The next morning he found himself in Victoria (some three hundred miles from Bali).

Moses Fonjeh was from Bali and had gone to Douala where he learned to drive and became a mechanic. There were others in Douala working at the port, on the railway, and like Moses driving for the Public Works Department (PWD). He was taken by the army and sent to a depot in Lagos.

Clement Ngu Ngwa had traveled from Bafut to the coast where he worked on one of German plantations. On one plantation Clement became a "motor mechanic and blacksmith," and spent five years and ten months in a Bota workshop. In 1939 he was unemployed and returned home to Bafut. "In1940 I showed my certificate and went to soldier work in 1941."

Thomas Go-oh Natang was originally from Bakossi but had worked as a house steward, or servant, for a Catholic mission. The priest at the mission station was Fr. Francis Woodman. Fr. Woodman became a British army chaplain. He remembered Thomas and sent him a telegram telling him to join the army. As a chaplain and an officer, Fr. Woodman was able to have a personal assistant, "a batman and steward." "I received a uniform and a gun but only served as a steward to Father," in North Africa.

One veteran, **Michael Mom of Kuk**, had learned to cook at Soppo, near Buea in the southwest, at the residence of Bishop Peter Rogan of the Catholic Mission. Unemployed in 1941, he enlisted at Bamenda. He was given a rifle "but was a cook."

Michael Fong, also from Kuk, a village near Bafmeng, on the road to Wum, is one example. When he was old enough he went to the coast and worked on German plantations at Buea and Miselle clearing brush. He joined the army at Victoria on 18 April 1942, training first at Victoria and then at Enugu in Nigeria.

Others who worked on the plantations from the Bafmeng area were James Ching, Gregory Che Yeh, Sextus Awa, and Mathias Tah.

Some Men Were Recruited in the Village, Chosen by the "Chief," or "Fon"

Simon Rela, of Bafmeng was one. Soldiers came to the chief's palace, and the chief was told that recruits were needed for the army. Twelve were chosen by the chief and given to the soldiers. At Bamenda, of the twelve, only two were chosen. From Bamenda they went to the coast for training.

Misseng Ngong was also from Bafmeng and had been a trader, carrying kola nuts to Ebi in Nigeria. Returning from a trip he was among a group the chief chose to send as possible recruits. "I stood there and was taken," he said.

Martin Kuh traded in kola nuts from Bafmeng, going as far as Kano in Nigeria. He joined at Victoria and not in the village.

Jacob Jaff of Kisong in Nso was a catechist for the Basel Mission in Jakiri. The Fon had been told by the government to supply men for the army. He was taken from the market on a day people had gone there to trade. At Victoria he signed his name.

Other Ex-Soldiers

Pa Akwe Linjo of Bali heard the government was asking "people to join the army if they liked." He decided to go.

Clement Sama of Bali worked on a plantation and then with an inspector of police who was stationed at Fontem. He joined the army at Tiko. "We were given uniforms and a gun. There were many of us".

Others from the Bali Area

Peter Ntungwen had learned carpentry and then painting with the PWD. An army officer came to Bamenda to recruit soldiers and he joined.

Michael Nketi from Njenka, Bali, heard that recruiters were at Bamenda, so he went and was taken.

Andreas Gemboh of Bawock, Bali, tried to join at Bamenda, "but his sister went to beg the officers to let him go because he was needed at home." He was released.

Pius Mbassong,of Gungong, Bali, had been a trader and worker on the Mamfe-Bamenda Road project. He saw an army officer at Bamenda and volunteered.

Among those men interviewed in 1999, at the Ex-Servicemen's Club, Limbe, a few spoke of special work they were given in the army.

Andrew Neng, from Wum was a plantation worker who became a military policeman.

Francis Njilifack, of Manyu and Bota, joined the army in 1943 and went to Nigeria, first to Aba and then Lagos. From there he went to Egypt as a driver and prison guard.

George Nkum Dinga had completed primary school at Soppo and was sent to Gold Coast (Ghana) to train with the Signal Corps.

Joseph Abang of Babanki Tungo, was working as a servant for a European in Nigeria when he joined the army at Calabar in 1942. He became a mess servant in the army.

Following recruitment and training, men of the British Cameroons were deployed, sent to the war front in India, Burma, and North Africa.

CHAPTER 4

Deployment to North Africa and Burma

That same morning (10 July 1943), in Lagos harbor, another chapter of the Second World War was opening. It was a damp grey day and a convoy of six troopships and four detroyers cut through the leaden waters of the lagoon and out towards the open sea. The men on the troopships would take part not in the war against fascism in Europe, but the one to defend the British Empire in Asia. They were the very first West African troops to set sail for Burma.

—Phillips, *Another Man's War*, 44–45

There were many ships and when we came to one place the ships divided, some going to North Africa and we to India. We took a train in India to Burma. That was in 1943.

—J. T. Ndikum

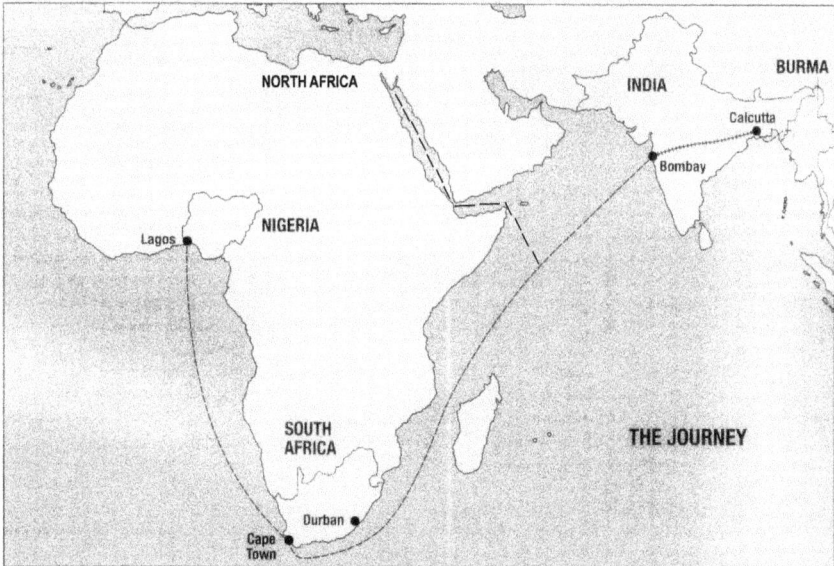

The sea route to Burma and North Africa

Transport of supplies and troops by sea to North Africa, India, and Burma was very dangerous. In March 1943 alone ten merchant ships totaling 62,000 tons were lost. In April there were another six. Admiral Sommerville's Eastern Fleet of a carrier, two battleships, and other ships were withdrawn. The Japanese then were joined by German submarines, and before the end of the year another fifty ships were sunk. It was only in January 1944 that the British were strengthened in the Indian Ocean by the arrival of larger ships.

In February 1944, a Japanese submarine sank the troop ship *Khedive Ismail,* which was sailing from Kenya to Colombo in Ceylon in a convoy of five ships. The convoy left Kilindini on 5 February 1944. On board were 996 members of the East African Artillery 301st Field Regiment, 271 Royal Navy personnel, 19 from the Women's Royal Navy Service (WRNS), 53 nursing sisters and matrons, and 9 First Aid nursing Yeomanry. They were escorted by an old cruiser the *Hawkins* and destroyers *Paladin* and *Petard.* On the afternoon of Saturday, 12 February, southwest of the Maldives, at 14:30 the Japanese submarine the *Addu Atoll I-27* appeared on the portside. Gunners opened fire. Commander Toshiaki fired four torpedoes and two hit the *Khedive Ismail* and she sank in three minutes. There were no lifeboats, only Carley floats.

The submarine hid below the survivors and the *Petard* attacked with depth charges, shell fire and torpedoes for two and a half hours. Only 20 men and 6 women survived; 1,220 men and 77 women died. There is a war memorial in Mombasa remembering the disaster. It was the third largest loss of life at sea during World War II.[1]

SS *Khedive Ismail.* See: Britisharmynurses.com

The 81st Division began to leave for India and Burma in April and May 1943. The 6th Brigade, about 12,000 men, was to leave on 31 July. The liners *Britanic*, *Largs Bay*, and *Tamaroa* were able to carry 8,528 of the troops. Another ship, the SS *California* came directly from the Clyde in Scotand to transport the rest.

CHAPTER 5

North Africa

By mid-1940 the war in Europe had spread to colonial Africa as Italy declared war on Britain. . . . Large numbers of African soldiers were required as uniformed labour in North Africa and the Levant.[1]

—David Killingray, *Fighting for Britain*

The African Auxiliary Pioneer Corps' (AAPC) primary mission was to provide logistical support for the British Eighth Army's campaign against the Germans and Italians in North Africa. African Pioneer companies repaired tanks, assembled trucks, served as dockworkers and built railway lines, roads and water pipelines. While AAPC companies had some combat training . . . their official role was to work behind the front lines.[2]

—Timothy Parsons, in *Africa and World War II*

Between 1940 and 1943 during World War II there was a series of battles fought for control of North Africa. The prize was control of the Suez Canal, a lifeline of the British Empire and access to the oil reserves of the Middle East.

Ex-soldiers from the British Cameroons spoke of their duties in North Africa. Most were assigned to guard prisoners of war, especially Italian soldiers captured after the Battles of El-Alamein.

Following is a description from the Australian War Memorial online of an Italian prisoner of war camp: "Camp 306 is an immense camp consisting of 24 sections each with several dozen tents and able to house 500 to 800 prisoners. In February 1942, 23 sections were occupied by Italian prisoners of war; 3 of these sections were reserved for officers."

"In total there were 301 officers: three lieutenant-colonels, seven majors, three priests, 34 doctors and 34 assistants to the officers."

"There were 700 Italian soldiers in each of the other 19 sections. In each section there are 60 tents. The men sleep on the sand and have two or three covers/blankets at their disposal. They have no complaints about the cold."

"The camp is situated in a desert region but has picturesque views of a lake and some mountains. The climate is healthy."

El-Alamein: Italian prisoners of war being led into a barbed-wire enclosure after the Second Battle of El-Alamein, November 1942. Farm Security Administration, Office of War Information Photograph Collection/Library of Congress, Washington, D.C. (digital file no. LC-USZ62-132809).

ITALIAN PRISONERS.

Thousands Interned in Palestine.

LONDON, Dec. 24.—Some of the many thousands of Italian prisoners captured by the British forces in the Western Desert have been sent to Palestine for internment. An internment camp has been established on the Central Judean plain, alongside a monastery. Two thousand prisoners were taken to the camp yesterday, after having been landed at Haifa on the previous day.

The Jerusalem correspondent of the Associated Press quotes an unnamed Australian soldier, watching the arrival of the Italian prisoners as saying: "If these are Mussolini's glorious legions old Musso is due for a sad disappointment."

The *West Australian* (Perth, WA)
26 December 1940

An example of a POW camp in North Africa has been documented by Australia. There was one camp for Italian prisoners of war at Gineifa, Egypt, not far from Suez in 1941. The photograph was taken from a passing train. Source: Australian War Memorial

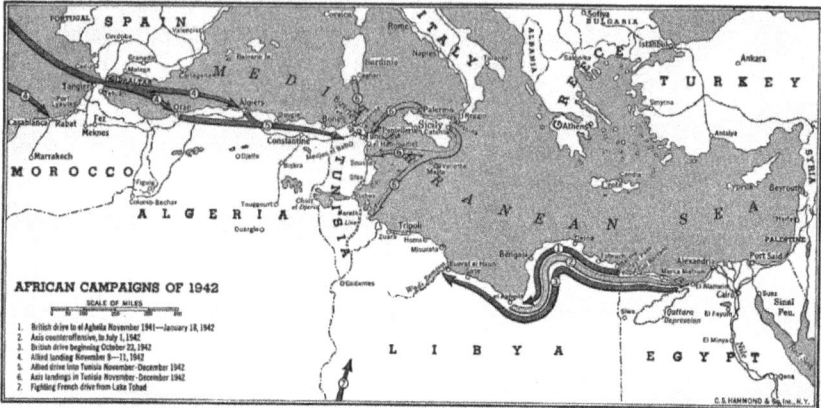

AFRICAN CAMPAIGNS OF 1942

SCALE OF MILES

1. British drive to el Agheila November 1941—January 18, 1942
2. Axis counteroffensive, to July 1, 1942
3. British drive beginning October 23, 1942
4. Allied landing November 8—11, 1942
5. Allied drive into Tunisia November-December 1942
6. Axis landings in Tunisia November-December 1942
7. Fighting French drive from Lake Tchad

21 December 1940. Men gathered in a field at Wady Sarar. Library of Congress Matson Collection: Eric and Edith Matson. Another camp was 35 km from Jerusalem.

1941. Italian Prisoners hear Christmas Mass in Jerusalem. *Catholic Freeman's Journal* (Sydney, NSW), 17 April 1942, p. 13

Italian Prisoners Hear Christmas Mass in Jerusalem.

By courtesy of the British Army in the Western Desert and the good offices of an English Army chaplain, large numbers of Italian soldiers heard their Christmas Mass in the holy city of Jerusalem.

Special midnight Masses were arranged for the prisoners, who also received holiday food prepared by a former New York hotel chef appointed specially to cook for them.

A second contingent of Fascist captives arrived in Palestine and marched through Haifa's streets. Many of them expressed surprise that Haifa was still standing, as they had thought the Italian air force had demolished the city.

An Italian corporal said Fascist troops in Egypt had known nothing of Italian reversals in the Greek campaign—"Catholic Herald."

"Two hundred prisoners per section work in the camp constructing paths around the tents etc. They work approximately 8 hours a day but do not work on Fridays or Sundays. They are paid 2 piastres per day, on top of their allowance of ten piastres: 10 one week and 5 the alternate week. The pay is paid regularly."

In February 1943 it was reported that: "No complaints about payments. Italians with the exception of officers, the men receive their pay and wages in cash. Italian officers receive 1 Egyptian pound in cash and the remainder is credited to their individual accounts."[3]

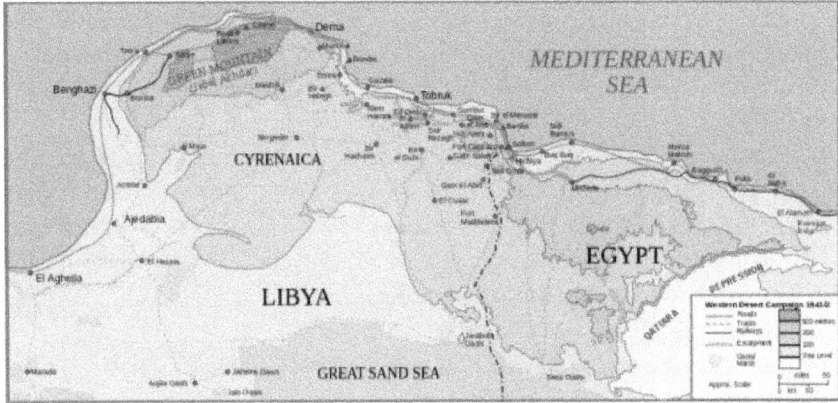

North Africa: Testimony of Men from the British Cameroons

Former soldiers from the British Cameroons spoke about their service in North Africa.

Thomas Go-oh Natang went first to Lagos where they took a ship to Cape Town, a journey that took three weeks. After a few nights in South Africa they continued for four weeks to the Red Sea and finally to Port Said and Cairo in Egypt. In North Africa they guarded prisoners of war. As steward to Captain Fr. Francis Woodman he traveled with father when he visited the African troops who guarded prisoners at places like Tobruk for six months, Tripoli for six months, and Dema for seven months. He was with Woodman when he went to visit the men at Benghazi "to see where the soldiers lived." They finally came to Alexandria when the war was over. A high note of his travels with the chaplain was a visit to Jerusalem. In his interview and that of others, it was clear how great an impression the visit to the Holy Land made on the men from British Cameroons.

Michael Fong of Kuk guarded prisoners for two years. They had a leave of seven days and chose to visit Jerusalem and Bethlehem. "I ben walka all Jerusalem."

Simon Rela of Bafmeng described taking a troopship to Egypt where they received further training and guarded captured German soldiers. He too went

with others and Fr. Woodman to Jerusalem and Bethlehem. It was Fr. Wood-
man who arranged for a catechist to be teaching those soldiers interested in
Baptism. Simon was prepared for six months and baptized at Kasserine by Fr.
Woodman.

Some, like **Gregory Che Yeh**,of Bafmeng, were given leave and took a train
to Jerusalem and Bethlehem for six days.

Another who visited Jerusalem with Fr. Woodman was **Sextus Awa**, also of
Bafmeng. He recalled spending one year guarding prisoners at Tobruk.

Pius Mbasong of Gungong, Bali, described the troopship reaching Suez and
then the men moving to Kasserine where they stayed for two months. He
remembered Tobruk and Benghazi and then going to Alexandria, where they
guarded prisoners. The prisoners were not only from North Africa but from the
war in Europe.

"They used to bring them across the Mediterranean Sea and we would be
guarding them. Some war prisoners were working on the roads while others
were to maintain what the war had damaged."

After one year, the men were give a leave of seven days. He also traveled with
Fr. Woodman to the Holy Land. Like others the visit to the land of Jesus made
a lasting impression.

Pius is one of a few who said he was among those who traveled to Italy. He
went to Naples and guarded prisoners of war who were transported to camps in
North Africa.

His impression of Cairo at the time was that it was a bad place where people
were "stolen," and there were people starving." "There was no food, nothing.
When they used to cut bread to give us the bits that fell to the ground they
would be picking them all up."

Pa Akwie Linjo of Bali remembered being among those who traveled to Italy
for prisoners. He also said that at some point they were on the "war front,"
where he killed some people: "I fired the gun and never knew if the soldiers
died. Perhaps they ran and died later." While in the army he spoke of an allowance of one pound ten shillings. About food, he said they were fed "free of
charge".

Peter Ntungwen, of Bali, remembered that the troopship left Lagos and
took 42 days before reaching Cape Town. After three days in Cape Town, it
took another two weeks to reach Aden, where the convoy of ships divided, with
some going to India and the rest entered the Red Sea and stopped at Port Said.
From there the troops went by train to Cairo. Peter describes training at Cairo
for three months before going to the "war front" at Tobruk. He was among
those who went to Sicily. "Then it was there that the Italians surrendered, and as
such we couldn't go further towards that side again. We went back as a garrison
troop. We gathered some war prisoners and went to "Grozza," and they were
settled there."

After some time he and his men returned to Cairo to rejoin his company.

Again Peter had an important experience with others visiting the Holy Land. In addition, he received his baptism as a Catholic. "When I was in Bamenda I had learned doctrine in the Catholic Church with Fr. Woodman, and when I joined the army I still met him at Benghazi in Libya, and it was there that he baptized me. Father Woodman was the Catholic chaplain to the Forces."

His memory was sharp about the commanding officers: Major Meeken and Captain J. G. Bell. "The man who was commanding the war in North Africa was a British head army commander, General Montgomery."

Misseng Ngong of Bafmeng was a corporal in the army. He spent time in West Africa serving in the Gold Coast and Gambia before going to North Africa to guard prisoners. He too went to Jerusalem on leave. He spoke of being prepared for baptism but on the day that the chaplain came to the camp to baptize some catechumens he was sent on guard duty.

Jacob Jaff of Nso talked about his time in North Africa. He said that they were trained to use a rifle but that he never killed anyone. He only guarded prisoners. Given leave, he traveled to Jerusalem with Fr. Woodman. Jacob was not a Catholic, but Fr. Woodman as chaplain used to move with them "and looked out for all the soldiers." He never saw him again.

The next chapter is about the war in Burma, where many interviewees in this book did their service. Africans served in what has been called "The Forgotten Army." It was found that only an estimated 50 percent of the British population "had a basic grasp" of the war in Asia. Yet the 14th Army included over a million soldiers from the Commonwealth, India, and Australia and divisions from West and East Africa; the 81st, 82nd, and the East African 11th. The 14th Army in 1944 and 1945 "fought a brutal, grueling war in the jungles of Burma."[4]

CHAPTER 6

Burma

I was in a Brigade, 4th Battalion, 81st Division. We sailed to South Africa in two weeks and then on to Bombay. We took a train in India to Burma. That was in 1943. . . . The war with the Japanese was "no small thing." Many people died. Sometimes we walked on blood.

—J. T. Ndikum, Bamenda, 14 July 2006

"You know, the real decisive factor is not going to be tactics," he declared, "it's is going to be the new West African Divisions who will be coming into this theatre." (Gifford had commanded in West Africa for some time and had the highest regard for these black troops.) They will be the answer to the Jap in jungle fighting."[1]

—Henry Maule, *Spearhead General*, 215

The 81 (West African) Division is frequently mentioned in the histories of the war in Burma but usually in general terms. . . . Yet the Division was unique in the story of the British Empire. It was the largest concentration of our African troops ever and it played a very significant part in the victory of the 14th Army over the Japanese in Burma.

—His Royal Highness, Prince Philip, in the Foreword of *War Bush*

African troops were first used in the East African campaign against the Italians, as Pioneer labor and garrison units in the Middle East, and then, after 1943, as combatants in Burma, now Myanmar, where they fought as complete formations within the Commonwealth forces.

A very good introduction to the experience of West Africans, including British Cameroonians, in Burma during World War II, is, again, Barnaby Phillips's book *Another Man's War*: "In December 1941 the Japanese invaded Burma. For the British, the longest land campaign of the Second World War had begun. 100,000 African soldiers were taken from Britain's colonies to fight the Japanese in the Burmese jungles. They performed heroically in one of the most brutal theatres of war, yet their contribution has been largely ignored."[2]

Burma is a country in South Asia that lies between India and China. There are mountains as high as 12,000 feet in the west. In the south there is the Bay of Bengal and the Andaman Sea. In the east there are more mountains. In the

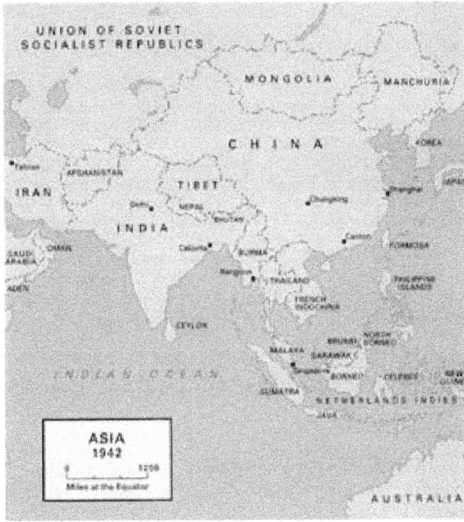

south east is Thailand. In the center there are plains, river valleys and deltas running north to south. The Irrawaddy and the Chindwin Rivers drain the west and the Salivan and Sittang the east.

From the nineteenth century Burma was part of Britain's colonial empire. Britain tried to govern Burma as part of India but failed. In 1937 Burma became a separate colony.

There was also an independence movement in Burma. Japan was to appeal to such movements in Asia, claiming that they came as liberators from the colonial control of European powers. Japan was also interested in the oil, rubber, tin, and rice of Burma. During World War II, Prime Minister Winston Churchill made it clear that both India and Burma were colonies of the British Empire and were to remain so after the war.

A week after the bombing of Pearl Harbor by Japan on 7 December 1941 and the entry of the United States into World War II, Japanese airplanes attacked an airfield south of Rangoon, the capital of Burma. The British were not prepared for war, and an invasion of Japanese ground forces began. In March 1942 British forces abandoned Rangoon and fell back to the border with India.

By 1940 one of the two supply lines remaining for the United States to send war material to the Nationalists fighting the Japanese in China went through Burma. It was an improved gravel highway from Lashio in Burma to Kunming in China. It was to secure this supply line to China and to prevent Japan invading India that an army was assembled to fight the war in Burma. Two divisions from West Africa were recruited. The Cameroonians who served in Burma were among the thousands of Commonwealth troops who supported the British attack on the invading armies of Japan.

According to David Killingray, when Italy entered the war, 10,000 West African troops were at sea en route to East Africa. In the end, West African forces were shipped home to guard against a possible Vichy threat. The Colonial Office to mid-1941 had two roles for African Colonial Forces (ACF). They were to serve as combatants and non-combatants in Africa. With the end of the threat from French colonies in Africa under the Vichy government, it was decided to use African troops in Asia.[3]

On 9 December 1942, the commander of the British army in India wrote to the War Office in London suggesting that West African soldiers be used to recapture Burma and Malaya. On 30 December, London agreed that, since there was no longer a threat of invasion in West Africa, they might be used. On 1 January 1943 the War Office notified West Africa that two divisions were needed to fight in Burma. This amounted to 56,000 men and perhaps more for support. They would become the 81st and 82nd Divisions.

On 1 January 1943 the War Office instructed General Headquarters (GHQ) West Africa to begin raising the 81st Division. It was formed on 1 March 1943 in Nigeria, followed two weeks later with orders for another division.[4]

The 81st had been raised in Southern Nigeria in March 1943 under Major General Christopher Woolner. The War Office informed the division that it was to be deployed to Burma. The division had to be prepared, but there was "no accepted doctrine for jungle warfare." There were no manuals. One had to work it all out "on the spur of the moment." Furthermore the nearby terrain was unsuitable for training based on jungle fighting. In memoranda Woolner emphasized "individual training" at "Battle School at Olake-Meje."[5]

Malcom Milne, in *No Telephone to Heaven*, writes of service in the RWAFF training soldiers of the 81st Division to handle "screw guns" as part of batteries going to Burma. The main task of training the batteries "was, of course, just as much a job of training ourselves as training our rank and file. . . . Our guns were 3.7 Howitzers which took to pieces for head portage and became known as 'screw guns.' They were later to play an honourable role in the Burma campaign. There was one very heavy load of over 300 lbs which was carried on a short stretcher by two of the strongest men in the unit."[6]

Naowa Omoigui wrote about the two divisions in a history behind the names of various Barracks in Nigeria.

The 81st Division under Major General C. G. Woolner, CB, MC, "consisted of the 3rd, 5th and 6th (West Africa) Brigades. The 3rd Brigade under Brigadier H. U. Richards comprised the 6th, 7th and 12th Nigerian Battalions. The 5th (West Africa) Brigade was entirely Ghanaian (Gold Coast). The 6th Brigade combined battalions from Nigeria, Gambia and Sierra Leone under Brigadier J. W. A. Hayes DSO."

The 81st Divison had many of the men from British Cameroon among their number.

"Between August 14th and November 8th, 1943, various Brigades of the 81st Division arrived in Burma and concentrated at Chiringa, which thus became the West African Base and Rear Headquarters. Barely after arrival, with no animals or vehicles in support, the Division was 'volunteered' by General Gifford, C-in-C Eastern Command, to advance independently of the main Arakan formation along the Kaladan River on the left, threatening the Japanese flank and their west-east lines of communication at Kanzauk Pass. General Slim regarded this area of operations as 'the dangerous spot in Arakan.' The axis of advance meant the Africans would have to totally rely on air re-supply—the first time an entire unit of that size would be deployed under such circumstances. The 81st created a jeep track through 75 miles of jungle from Chiringa to Satpaung (nicknamed 'West Africa Way') and constructed airstrips along the Kaladan River."

At the end of March 1945, the 81st Division was withdrawn from Burma and left for India. "They had suffered 74 killed, 343 wounded and 21 missing in the Arakan campaign. Later on, in August 1944, the 3rd (West Africa/Nigerian) Brigade of the Chindits, under Brigadier A. H. Gillmore was also withdrawn from Burma. Brigadier P. M. Hughes later replaced Gillmore. They were reunited with the main 81st Division on March 20th, 1945, in India."[7]

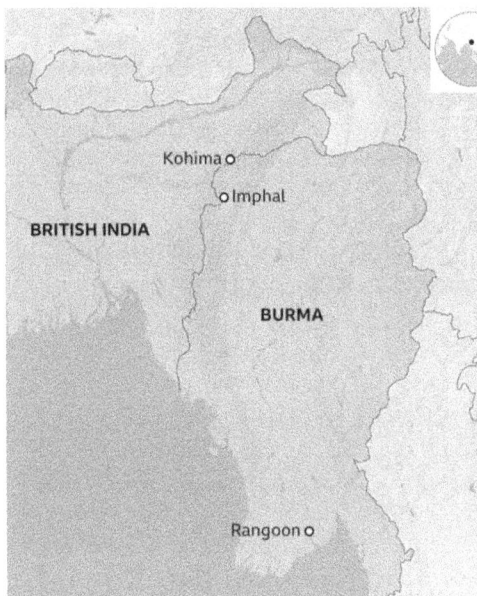

U. S. Army Center of Military History

Lord Louis Mountbatten, Supreme Allied Commander, seen during his tour of the Arakan Front in February 1944.
Source: WikiCommons

Plans were underway for the division to fight the Japanese in Malaya when the Japanese surrendered. In May 1946, the 81st Division returned to Nigeria.

The 82nd West African Division had been dispatched to India in July 1944, to join the XV Corps as part of the "Fourteenth Army" under Slim. "It was mainly Nigerians of the 82nd Division that achieved the subsequent clearance of Japanese forces from the coastal belt of the south Arakan. In April, the Division, with the East African 22nd Brigade now under command, advanced south from Tamandu. By the end of May, Kindaungyyi, Taungup, and Sandoway had been captured. The end was in sight."

"Both the 81st and 82nd Divisions achieved their duties with excellence. . . . According to the Commonwealth Graves Commission, total numbers of lost, killed and wounded were 438 for the 81st (WA) Div and 2,085 for the 82nd (WA) Div. In addition to those buried in jungle tracts, many Nigerian graves remain in cemeteries of Burma like the Dalet Chaung near Tamandu and the Taukyan War Cemetery. Others are remembered at the War Memorial in Rangoon."

Barnaby Phillips describes the departure of the 81st Division for Burma on 10 July 1943:

Major General
Christopher Woolner
Permission: National Portrait
Gallery, London

It was a damp grey day and a convoy of six troopships and four destroyers cut through the leaden waters of the lagoon and out towards the sea. They were the very first West African troops to set sail for Burma. It was the 81st Division of the Royal West African Frontier Force, 28,000 men. It was an operation that was to involve three additional convoys and several weeks.

The 81st was under the command of Major General Christopher Woolner, a 49 year old veteran of World War I. According to John Hamilton he was known to his peers as "Kit." To the Europeans of the 81st as "Father" and to the Africans as "Pappa." He had a reputation for being a stern disciplinarian, trim and smartly dressed and always clean-shaven. Woolner had clear blue eyes, and could deliver a cold stare of disapproval to soldiers and officers alike when he felt they had fallen short of his exacting standards. He had served five years in West Africa. He worried that his troops and officers had little time for preparation.

It was General Woolner who chose the divisional badge sewn into each soldier's uniform: a black spider on a yellow background. The spider represented Ananse, from Ashanti mythology. It was a cunning animal spirit that could change form and overcome larger enemies. He hoped that his men would take his choice to heart.[8]

Military chaplains accompanied the troops. "Every morning after breakfast, a Catholic priest held a well-attended prayer session on the deck, always starting with a rediton of 'Onward Christian Soldiers.' Never mind that many of the soldiers were Muslims they joined him singing with gusto."

Formation badge for 81st West
African Division. The divisional
commander, General Woolner,
chose the black spider design, which
represented "Gizzo" or "Anase," a
figure in Ashanti mythology who
could overcome his enemies
through guile.

After stopping in Cape Town and Durban, the convoy sailed on to Bombay on 14 August, "a soggy day of low skys." "Thousands of West Africans in khaki uniforms filed off the ships onto the quayside next to the Gateway to India." The troops marched from the docks to the railway station, the Victoria Terminus. The troops left Bombay and climbed an escarpment to Nasik and from there marched to their camp three miles away at Deolali. They slept in bell tents, holding six men.

The first of the 81st Division waited four months for the entire division to assemble. The last ships only arrived in November 1943.

A new commander of the 14th Army, General William Slim, arrived on 17 September 1943. His task was to prevent a Japanese invasion of India and reconquer Burma. The army was made up of India soldiers. The British and African troops amounted to about 100,000 of the total 500,000.

"He set out to restore morale among the diverse force." He emphasized better hygine, food and "Logistics." Slim remained four days with the 81st Division in the Deolali camp.

In mid-November the 81st Division began to prepare for a long trip to the frontier with Burma. They traveled by train for five days and nights to Calcutta.

In December, the West African soldiers boarded troopships which took them across the Bay of Bengal to the port of Chittagong, about 60 miles north of the frontier. They changed their khaki uniforms for "olive-green battle dress, green jumpers and long rubber capes."

General Sir George James Giffard.
Source: Wiki Creative Commons

One of their commanding officers was Major Robert Murphy. He came from Greenock, a grey shipbuilding town on the banks of the River Clyde in Scotland. His parents prayed he might become a Catholic priest but instead he went to Glasgow University where he graduated in 1936. "But he put a promising medical career on hold" at the beginning of the war.

The troops packed up and marched through the Bengali countryside until the reached a railway. The road by train for 30 miles to a place called Dohazari. "On the horizon they could see blue mountains covered in a thin film of mist. They marked the border between India and Burma, the direction they were heading in." From there, buses took them southwards to a little town of Chiringa. It was there around Chistmas Day 1943 that the 81st Division set up its headquarters.

The 81st Division was to be part of some of the worst fighting in World War II in a narrow strip of land along 400 miles of the Bay of Bengal called the "Arakan." There the West Africans entered an area of dense forests and mountains. During the monsoon season from May till October it was one of the wettest areas of the world.

General Slim decided that the 81st Division was to fight its way down the Kaladan Valley on the eastern flank of the main force. General Woolner led the 81st forward. One effort was to clear a jeep track 75 miles long through wild jungle hills and ravines, from Chiringa in India, to a village on the Kaladan River. When the track was opened on 17 January 1944, General Woolner praised the "enthusiasm and endurance" of his men. The 81st called the track the "West African Way." With this effort the West Africans began their service in Burma.

Barnaby Phillip's story continues to describe the hardships of the Burma campaign and of the 81st Division in the fight.

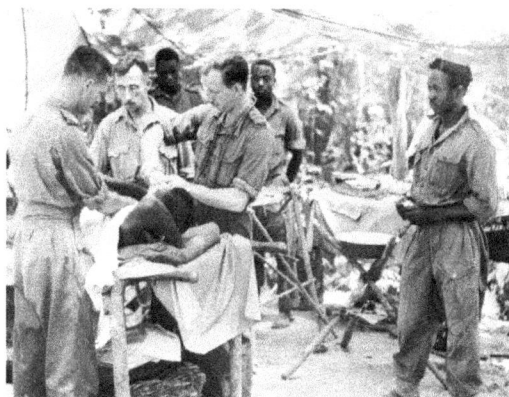

August 1944: Doctors care for a wounded 81st (WA) Division soldier in an improvised operating theatre in the Kaladan Valley, Burma.
Source: RWAFF photographer: public domain

Some Former Soldiers from the British Cameroons
Who Served in Burma in World War II

Joseph Ndikum was in the 81st Division in 1943 when they entered a troopship. Their destination was never disclosed. They traveled for six weeks by ship, first to Cape Town before reaching Bombay in India. After three weeks, they went to Madras (Chennai) for two months and then on to Calcutta. While in Madras he was a driver for a general he calls "Warner," but it was most likely General Woolner, the top officer of the 81st Division. Joseph was a soldier in the 4th Brigade. In the dry season they began their march into Burma. He remembers being supplied with food dropped by airplanes at a place he called "Cox Bazaar." Then the 81st Division attacked. He was wounded in the hand. "I was there with some of the people from my place. Among them were Mukochu, Kanoi and Njatoh. All the boys died there but I came back. My number in the army was 38439."

George Nkum Dinga was from Esu in what is now the Northwest Region. He served in the Signal Corps in North Africa, India, and Burma which is unusual for those interviewed; that is, to have served in North Africa and Burma.

According to his Discharge Card, he left the service a corporal and was awarded the Burma Star, the Defense Medal, and the Africa Star, which supports what he said.

William Neufville served in Burma but was not from British Cameroons but Liberia. He was with the WAFF divisions on the troopships to India and Burma where he was an ammunition carrier for a tank division in the armored car brigade which he calls the "Highland Brigade."

Peter Nji of Kuk spent time with the Kru people of Ivory Coast and Liberia but did not explain that information. Peter said that the ship left Lagos and made a stop in Durban after Cape Town in South Africa on the way to India. In Burma he was given work to collect the food and war material dropped to the Division from the air by parachute.

James Ching of Bafmeng thought that joining the army was not to see the world but to do "soldier work," stressing the seriousness of going to war. This fits with Joseph Ndikum's comment in the title that going to Burma was "No Small Thing," a great understatement, especially in Pidgin English.

James was a runner in Company A, Battalion 8. In Burma he remembers sleeping on the ground in what the military sometimes call "foxholes."

Mathias Tah, also a Bafmeng man, joined the army at the beginning of 1941 and did his training in Gold Coast (Ghana), where he was baptized. In 1943 they were sent to Lagos where they joined the troopships to India, Burma, and the War.

"For 1944–45 we were in Burma and then returned to India and in 1946 went back to Lagos and Victoria."

Martin Kuh was among the many soldiers from Bafmeng. He joined at Victoria in 1942, did his training in Enugu in Nigeria, and shipped out to Burma. He remembers sleeping on board ship for about two months. "We just went when war was almost finished. I just held a gun in my hand."

Clement Ngu Ngwa of Bafut enlisted in 1941, training first at Bota before going to Sierra Leone. He was a mechanic. From there he was sent to India and Burma, rising in rank to corporal in the Nigeria Regiment. His Discharge Card noted he was a blacksmith and mechanic with the 4th Battalion.

Clement Sama of Bali joined at Tiko. Like Clement Ngwa, he too went first to Sierra Leone for training before going by ship to Cape Town and Burma. "I was an infantryman for five years. What I remember of Burma was that it was too cold."

CHAPTER 7

Interviews with Ex-Servicemen from Cameroons

Tepe and Dinga were boys of the Bamenda Highlands in the British Cameroons. Dinga was from the village of Esu and had done some primary schooling at Bamenda before completing his Standard 6 at Soppo, near Buea Mountain at the coast. Now he was working at the Bamenda station for a British officer.

One morning his friend Tepe trekked along the ridge of the escarpment between Bamenda and the East Cameroun border. He followed the footpaths leading to Bamenda from the Santa Tea Plantation and the road to Pinyin and places south through the great forests to the creeks and the coast 300 miles away.

He approached the old German fort overlooking Bamenda. The Fort was now occupied by the offices of the British Station.

It was the dry season. It was a cold morning. He was barefooted, wearing khaki shorts and a torn short-sleeved shirt; his school uniform.

Passing the Station he saw the Union Jack flying above the brick walls of the fort. There were a few horses, a dust-covered Land Rover and an old Bedford lorry.

He saw no Europeans, but there were several African soldiers and a few police at attention outside. His friend Dinga was a houseboy for one of the white officers and so he knew something about the English and their behavior.

—R. O'Neil, *A First Encounter*

I shall never recapture the feeling of excitement I had that morning when I boarded the train heading for Jerusalem, the "Holy City," the city of David, the city paved with gold. This vision of Jerusalem was in my mind as the train moved swiftly towards the city. To me there was little difference between the Jerusalem in Palestine and the Golden Jerusalem in heaven. The heavenly Jerusalem was always more real to me than the Jerusalem that existed in Palestine. I felt I knew the heavenly city.[1]

—Bilad Kaggia, *Roots of Freedom*

Bamenda

Bamenda, the capital of the Northwest Region, is a city whose area had a population of 594,000 inhabitants in 2023. It was a place that missionaries working in the countryside visited frequently from Kom, Wum, Bafmeng, Widekum, and Batibo in the 1960s, '70s and '80s. The home of Mr. Joseph Tepe Ndikum was a favored stop before heading back to our mission station. In those days one drove over very rough roads to an old section of the town, a street lined with small shops and stores and homes in a section called Abaqua. On the right was the home of J.T., a small covered veranda and a shop with small items for sale along with beer and soft drinks, and often palm wine from the countryside. We sat on the porch near to the road. Usually he offered a Coca-Cola and we talked of work, the need for J.T. to transport food to St. Bade's College in Kom country or building supplies elsewhere. He loved to talk of the old days and some of the tough jobs he did, especially about working for various missions and some of the old missionaries he knew. When prompted, he would talk about his military service in the British army during World War II.

I first met Joseph Tepe Ndikum in December 1965. Matthew Nabben, a Mill Hill Missionary and the parish priest of the Catholic Mission at Mankon, Bamenda, asked him to carry me with my baggage over the old road to Njinikom, my first station. We sat up front in the cab of his Bedford lorry as we moved up Mbingo Hill and then into the valleys of the Kom people. At the village of Sho one could look across the valley to see the red oxide roofing of the old Njinikom church and mission house. Kom would be home for the next six years. It was during this time that J.T. and I became more acquainted. He was known simply as "J.T." in those years. Our friendship continued for more than forty years.

And so it was not news that many Africans, including Cameroonians, had served in the British army during World War II. Joseph was an ex-serviceman who enjoyed sharing his wartime experiences in Africa, India, and Burma. In addition, the rector of St. Anthony's parish at Njinikom in 1965 was Captain Francis Woodman. Father Woodman had served as a chaplain with the Cameroonian troops in North Africa. His head-man in the mission was Thomas Go-oh Natang, who had been in the army and had served as Fr. Woodman's orderly, in North Africa.

Many years later, Mr. Ndikum visited his daughter and her family in the United States. The May 9, 1996, issue of the *Capital Weekly* (Augusta, Maine) ran this headline under "Capital Profile":

Heading: *J.T. meets grandchildren during first trip to America.*

Mr. Ndikum admitted to the reporter that he did not receive a veteran's pension from the British Government, but yet *"he remains fiercely proud of his military service, so proud that he still wears his World War II cap and jacket. The jacket is adorned with four military commendations. Tepe brought the jacket and cap with him to America. He wore it to the State House, where he met with Governor Angus King and presented him with coffee from Cameroon."* During that visit he was introduced to the Legislature and received a standing ovation. According to his daughter, during the ovation, her father was in tears as he gave a military salute to the members of the Legislature.[2]

The following are taken from interviews with the ex-soldiers. Most of these interviews were with people in the Bamenda Division over three years, from 1988 to 1991. Today the area is the Northwest Region of the Cameroons.

Mr. Joseph Tepe Ndikum with Governor Angus King, Augusta, Maine, May 1996.[3] Source: Mrs. Brigitte Ndikum Nyada

Interviews

In 1988, I was in Balinyonga replacing the parish priest, Jeremiah Doona, who had taken ill and had returned to Ireland for treatment. Balinyonga was the chiefdom that welcomed the German explorer, Eugen Zintgraff, and his caravan in 1889. Zintgraff is the first recorded European to visit the Cameroon Grassfields from the Atlantic coast. It became a mission station for the Basel Mission prior to World War I. In 1988, St. Francis Xavier Mission of the Roman Catholics had also been in Balinyonga for many years.

In late 1988 and 1989, I moved to Bafmeng, a mission on the road from Njinikom to Wum. In both stations there was opportunity to interview many elders.

Not all interviews were arranged. Some were by chance. There might be a stranger we met on a local road. Other times arrangements were made to meet with interviewees in their compounds. Occasionally a gathering was arranged for a few people to be interviewed in a school classroom or a meeting house. In those days I carried a leather bag with bound school notebooks from Nigeria. Usually Mr. Bernard Forkwa assisted with a tape recorder.

Bamenda Division in 1939. Detail from Buea Archive map.

Fr. Remo Gulinelli, rector, a priest of the Diocese of Modena in Italy, who was a missionary for many years in Cameroon, with some of the first Catholics in 1978. Bali Catholic Mission was first opened around World War I and then as a parish with a resident priest in 1953 by Bernard Kolkman, a Mill Hill Missionary.
Photo: © R. O'Neil

The stories told by many of those Cameroonians are given here.

Pius Mbasong, *Gungong, Bali, 8 August, 1988*

One veteran I met by chance in a small mimbo shed on the Bali-Batibo Road was Pius Mbasong. Pius said that he spoke of his experiences on return home but very soon his people said "we have heard enough!" And so "I hardly spoke again about what I had seen."

... As a small boy I stayed here, and in 1920 I started attending school in government school Bali. That school was opened in 1920. After I left the school I was doing some trade. I used to go to Victoria, buy things, and would come and sell here. At the time I was doing trading I had already got married. The name of my first wife was Magoh. I have five children with her. I have a second wife. Her name is Julia Janga. I have only two wives.

After trading I later worked with the Public Works Department (PWD) on the Mamfe road. We were many from Bali there. We worked on the Manyu Bridge. When one wanted to work there, he would first go there and tell the people and they would write his name and he would join the work. By the time I was going to Ekom they were surveying the road, and because my trade was not profitable I decide to go and do that work. I stayed there for two years. After that work I went to the army in 1940.

Before I joined the army I went and met the officer at Bamenda and my name was written and I was sent to a doctor. After that we left for training at Victoria; from there to Calabar and from Calabar to Lagos. We had our training in Lagos for twelve months. The officer who was in charge of the training at Lagos was Major Brown. There was also Sergeant Lezatt. I was a corporal and had twenty-three men.

When we were going for the war we entered the ship at Lagos. The name of that ship was *Omboro*. It was a Cameroonian ship. Then we left from Lagos, reached Sierra Leone, Freetown, and then reached Gambia. We left again from Sierra Leone and went straight to Cape Town in South Africa. From there we stayed in the ship one month and then reached the Red Sea. We crossed the Red Sea and stopped there. Japan and India were on one side and those with Germany were one side. That ship later took us and we reached Suez. It was there that we dropped down and went to Kasserine. We were there for two months and then we came out and started the war. We fought in Tobruk, Addi, Dena, Benghazi. Then we went down to Tripoli and then came to Alexandria. It was there that we kept war prisoners and we were guarding then. We were put on the war front and we were shooting guns. I as a corporal was the one commanding my people. The war captain was there to inform me of all things and we would be shooting. When we reached Tobruk we captured the Germans. As we were there many people died. We left to Tripoli and then to Alexandria, where we were guarding war prisoners. They used to bring them across the Mediterranean Sea and we would be guarding them. Some war prisoners were working on the road while others were to maintain what the war had damaged.

We were there for one year and we were given a casual leave of seven days and we went to Jerusalem. There we traveled to all the places. We went to Bethlehem where Jesus was born and saw it. We also saw River Jordan and I also "washed" in the water. I also went to where they caught Jesus. We reached the Garden of Eden. They used to go and show us all these places. Captain Francis Woodman was the Catholic chaplain. There were two chaplains. One for the Catholics and the other for the Presbyterians. I cannot remember the name of the Presbyterian chaplain. You know it is almost forty years from then and I cannot more remember his name.

I entered the house that Jesus built in three days. In that house there was a Catholic Church, the Orthodox. There are all churches inside. If one is a "Mamado" (Muslim) he would go there or what type of church you will find it there and get the father and he would bless you.

We were baptized by the father inside that church.

I didn't go to India. We made four years at the war front. We had gone to Italy to take war prisoners to Africa. We used to travel with war prisoners inside a ship. In Italy I had gone to Naples.

As the war ended we were given our pay arrears. The money was too small and when I came I gave it to my father. I did no business. Then I had to leave for Victoria afterwards and worked in the motor transport, Moliwe, to look after the motors. Many of us soldiers who came back were there. Some were night watchmen and some were headmen. I don't know if the government had attempted making the war returnees farmers here in Bali.

We came here and had our meeting of ex-soldiers, and anytime the government wanted to come, say the DO from Bamenda, we would salute him and do everything.

I got married to my second wife when I came back. I have sent all my children to school. I have sent seven of them and they have all completed school. One is a commissioner of police Bamenda, the other one is a headman in Bertoua, and two are in Victoria.

When I returned I met one elder and wanted to tell him all the things we had at war and Jerusalem and he told me that I should not tell him anything and that he has not even been in that place and I stayed quiet.

In Jerusalem I saw the place where Jesus was naked on the cross where he was buried and the people who were put there to guard him were sleeping. If you go there and see you will think that they are people.

At Bethlehem I also saw where Jesus was born where they have hung those two lights. That place is very nice. We were to Cairo. That place is a bad place.

Pa Akwie Linjo, *Bali, 3 August 1988*

My name is Akwie Linjo. I was born around 1930 (?) in Mbembe-Mesaje in Nkambe. My father's name was Sisoh Equoh and my mother's name was Nemie Chumbe. My mother left from Akoh village and then came and got married to my father in Aboseh Village.

When I was a child I used to follow my parents to the farm. That was the only thing I did during my childhood. I never went to school because by then there were no schools. Only my small brothers went to school when schools were later introduced.

At the age of about 22 years my father gave me a wife. I stayed with her for about five years and then left and joined the army. As an army officer I went to Calabar, Cairo, and Egypt. We had passed through South Africa before going to Egypt. I also went to Italy and even reached Jerusalem.

I managed to join the army because when we heard about the war the government asked people to join the army if they liked. So because we were determined to save the state from the Germans I decided to go and join the army. There, some of the people who controlled us were Captain Wesi from Britain, Major Boor, who later was at United Africa Company (UAC) Victoria, now Limbe. He used to call us up and grant us a party whenever an anniversary of the end of the war came. We used to eat and drink during such parties. There was also Commander Deisi, who was Scottish.

When we were in the war front I killed up to six people. I cannot even count those that I shot and perhaps they died without knowing because they used to run and perhaps died later.

When we killed a person, his friends would pick up the corpse.

At the war front or rather when serving in the army we had just an allowance. We had no salary. The allowance was 1 pound 10 shillings. About food: we were fed free of charge.

After we were discharged from the war front and later the army I became a custom officer at Fernando Po after which I became an army officer (militaire) and served in Yaoundé and Ngaoundere.

The experience I had from the war was that I was taught how to use a gun and even went and reached Jerusalem that I used to hear about in the Bible.

The wife I married left me because she said that I have no work and do not have any money. She left for another man. All the children I had with her are with her. The man she married she thinks has much money. I did not take back the bride-price paid and that is why I still think that she is my wife. She even paid me a visit here in Bali and stayed for a month and told me about the death celebration for her father. When she was going back I gave her money and again paid her transport to go back to our place.

I have two medals that have been given me. There is a War Medal 1939–45 and a War Defense Medal

Moses Fonjeh, Bali, 10 August 1988

My name is Moses Fonjeh. I was born at Banyo when my father was an army officer there during the German time. His name was Fonjeh. My mother was

Menah. She was a daughter of Bali here. When I was a boy I just used to be moving with my father since he was working.

When I was then a big boy I was serving in the houses of some German whitemen. Later I left and learnt mechanic driving at Douala. I was working there after I knew my work and was captured and put into the army as a driver in the 1939 war.

I was driving at Public Works, Douala, and then it was from there that I was caught and forced to be a driver in the army. Then we were taken to Port Harcourt and from there to Lagos. When I retired I came here. Then the Highways called me and it was with them that I was working. The money I brought from there I built a house at Mamfe with it. When I built that house in Mamfe I was staying inside and working with the Highways.

Before I went to the army I had got married and was staying in Douala with my wife. The name of my wife is Josephine Busong. I had three children with her but one died and two are left. One is overseas studying and one is at home with her husband.

When I retired from the army my people "been look me fine" because I came back with a better rank. I was a sergeant. Now I am receiving my government pension here at Bali from the government. When I was working in Lagos, Nigeria, they used to pay us 1-10/ as soldiers.

I was born during the First World War. I never attended school. It was in 1920 that we were caught and put in a school here but since my father later died I was annoyed and left the school. It was the government school that I attended. By then Dr. Villauer was gone.

I stayed in Douala for about seven years in the Bali Quarter because the people had their quarter there. The quarter-head there was Martin Ambe. There were many Bali people there working. We were working in the ships, on the railway, and others worked with the PWD.

I was baptized when I was a small child by the time my father was still in the army. I was baptized in the Basel Mission Church at Bangante.

When I was at Douala I used to attend the church. By then there was a big Basel Mission Church there.

As a driver in Douala I used to go to Kribi and other places. We used to carry government property from Wouri to other places. I used to transport materials (irons) in many big vehicles. The road by then was very bad. From Douala to Yaoundé we had two lorries on the way; one at Yapoma and the other at Sanaga. We even used to sleep in such lorries when we were many vehicles at a time.

In the army I used to be at the depot. That army was called the West African Frontier Force. There were so many people from all over West Africa there. At Lagos there were people from other places in West Africa and we used to move "for different camps," and used to carry materials and soldiers too.

Lagos by then was nice but not as today. One part of it by then was "bush." When I was there the small leave that was given was not enough for me to come right here. By then everywhere people were afraid of war so it was hard to be moving so much. At Lagos soldiers were just waiting and guarding the country.

Pa Andreas Gemboh, *Bawock, Bali, 31 August 1988*

My name is Andreas Gemboh. I was born at Bawock. My father was Boke Kama and my mother was Njadeg. My father had come from Bangante. My father had died when I was a very small child. After he died I remained with my mother and after some time she said that since my father had died and people were troubling her she would go somewhere and be staying there. Then she left and went to the East of Cameroon and left me here. She went there and was staying with one of her relatives. When she went I was staying here with Veronica Kwende, my elder sister. Then we stayed and when I grew and was a man I went and joined work and we constructed the Mamfe-Bamenda Road. I had joined the work when they were at Itoke and had left the work when the road had reached Timben. The overseer there that time was one man from Lagos, Mr. Pouba. Our headman was Stephen from Bahop. When I left the work Mr. Pouba said that I was to go with him to his country. Then they said that they were going to Kumba to take work material. While there they were recruiting people into the army for the Hitler war. I said they should also send me to go and carry the material but they refused and said I cannot go there (because of the recruitment going on).

As Mr. Pouba said that I should not go there, I decided to tell him that my father had just died and that I have to go and see the death celebration before coming back. He told me that if I go I shouldn't stay too long there and I accepted.

Then I left there and went to Bamenda and joined the army. When my sister heard that I had joined the army she came up to Bamenda. We were at the barrack, marching. . . . They wanted to write her name and told her she would be receiving money. But she refused. By then we had already cleaned our heads (had their heads shaved), but the army uniform was removed from my body and my sister took me away and we came down here to the village.

Clement Sama, *Bali, Monday, 29 August 1988*

I was born in 1922 at Baligham. My parents were Bande Key and Luma. . . .

I never went to school but went out to work on a plantation at Tiko, wrapping bananas. Later I became a laborer and carrier with an inspector of police called Mr. Trimbell who was stationed in Fontem. We traveled as far as Nso trying to catch smugglers. That was in 1939. I joined the army at Tiko. We were given uniforms and a gun. There were many of us. Our company was in the

Nigeria Regiment 4th Battalion. We went to Sierra Leone and then to Cape Town and finally to Burma. I was an infantryman for five years. What I remember of Burma was that it was too cold.

I came back to Lagos, but my savings book was stolen and I lost all my money.

When I returned to Cameroon I became a court messenger at Bali. I am a Mohammedan and married to two wives.

My good friend is J. T. Ndikum.

Peter Ntungwen, *Bali, 8 August 1988*

My name is Peter Ntungwen. I was born in 1922 in this quarter Mbang-wung. My mother was Debiga and my father was Nforgfuh. My mother was from Tezeh.

As I was a small child we used to set traps and catch birds and animals. After all these I left here in 1934 and with my elder brother to Nkambe where he was working as a court clerk. There I started attending school where we were taught using plantain leaves and a bamboo splitter. There were no exercise books by then. That school in Nkambe was run by the Baptist Mission, and teachers were brought from Victoria to teach us. I don't remember the names of those teachers.

Later we were transferred to Batibo in 1936. We stayed there 1936–37 and then we went back to Bamenda. Then I left school and learned carpentry. I was taught that work by one Mr. Fielding. He was a Bali man. After I learned the carpentry for three years, I was unable to have a job. So I had to learn painting for about three years at Bamenda with PWD. After that the war broke out in 1939. It was one Calabar man who had taught me that painting work.

I had joined the army when an army officer came to Bamenda to recruit soldiers. So I left that work with PWD and joined the army in 1940. Then we were taken down to Victoria. From there to Calabar, from Calabar to Kano, from Kano we came back to Lagos and we stayed there for about two months and then we joined the ship and went overseas. When we left Lagos we stayed for 42 days before reaching Cape Town. We stayed there for three days and then left for Aden and took two weeks, day and night.

It was there that we divided, some people were going through the Ocean to India, and those of us who were going to the Middle East entered the Red Sea and came out at Port Said and took a train to Cairo. We were trained there for three months. Then we left for Tobruk, where we entered the war. We fought there and later went down to Dena and from Dena to Benghazi, from Benghazi to Tripoli and from Tripoli to Sicily. Then it was there that the Italians surrendered and as such we couldn't go further towards that side again. We went back as a garrison troop. We gathered some war prisoners and went to Grozza and they were settled there and we were sent to Taravive to stay there. By that time we couldn't know where our company was. We were there for three months and then left for Cairo and joined our company.

Then we were preparing to go to Japan after that war had finished. We prepared for two weeks and then Japan surrendered with the two atomic bombs that were dropped by America. So we couldn't go to Japan again since they surrendered. So we stayed for some months and were sent to West Africa. We never again passed through South Africa but through Gibraltar before arriving in West Africa. It took us fifteen days to reach Lagos again. At Lagos we went to the demobilization camp at Ekeja and we were given rest of seven days. And we went to Lagos town to spend these days there.

When we were in Taravive we were given a holiday of seven days which we took and went to Jerusalem. We visited where Jesus was nailed to the cross. We also visited Bethlehem and had climbed right up and were seeing the Dead Sea below. We had entered a big church in Jerusalem. The floor is still ancient, it has not been cemented. We were even shown where Jesus was buried. From there we went back to Taravive.

At the war we were commanded by one Major Meeken and Capt. J. G. Bell and other officers. The man who was commanding the war in North Africa was a British head army commander, General Montgomery.

As we were coming back we had reached Lagos, went to Ekeja, to rest for one week. It was a sort of holiday given us. From there we joined a train for Port Harcourt. From there we took a ship back to Victoria. From Victoria, now Limbe, we took a vehicle to Bamenda and then we scattered.

Before we were disbanded we were paid our money at Lagos. The amount of money varied with the grades of the soldiers. Some took 70 pounds. The money they gave us to rest at Lagos was about 20-something pounds.

As I came back with my own money I divided it to my family. Then I stayed and was unable to have work. Then I left and went to Bamenda. One Mr. Fox from the CDC (Cameroon Development Corporation) came up and said he needed all classes of work people and then I joined as a carpenter. He took me to the CDC and I worked there for fourteen years. From there I joined the West Cameroon Development Agency as a carpenter, this time as a foreman. I was supervising the work. Then in 1972 I resigned and came up. When I reached I built this house and now I am doing farming.

When I was in Bamenda I had learned doctrine in the Catholic Church with one Fr. Woodman, and when I joined the army I still met him at Benghazi in Libya and it was there that he baptized me. Father Woodman was the Catholic chaplain to the Forces. I don't know the Presbyterian chaplain who was also there. I knew Fr. Woodman because we had been in Bamenda with him. When I returned from the war, my people were very happy because we came. Some used to visit me and I would be telling them the stories of that place. We had come back with our complete uniform and as we told the stories of the war we also showed them the uniform and the pictures that were snapped. So we dashed our brothers with those clothes and shoes we brought.

I got married to my only wife at the Tiko Catholic Church. I am with her now. I had four children with her but one died and now I have three of them with her. The first of the children is at the University of Yaoundé in the Faculty of Letters and Social Sciences. He is Martin Ntungwen.

As I came home I settled and I'm doing farming together with my wife, and it is from there that I am able to earn a living. I also do carpentry but that is only occasionally.

The money I brought from the army I did a bit of trading with. I traded in clothes. I was selling clothes from Bamenda to Nkambe. I also used to buy gun powder from Calabar, brought it and sold it here. We used to pass through Mamfe before going to Calabar. It took eight days to come back from Calabar.

Apart from what I learned at Nkambe on plantain leaves I also attended Bamenda Government School. When we left Nkambe we went to Batibo and from Batibo we went to Bamenda. There was no school at Batibo at the time. I completed Standard 4 at the Bamenda Government School. One of our teachers was Mr. Mbou. They were people from Mamfe and Calabar. They used to teach us arithmetic, songs, writing, and so on. Since that time I have never done any book work in any office. Immediately after I completed the school in Bamenda I joined that carpentry work.

Excerpts from his documents:
Catholic Soldiers Vade Mecum
Name: Peter Ntungwen
Army No.: 206856
Home Mission: Bamenda
Baptism: 16 August 1943, at Benghazi, by Fr. Woodman
Easter Duty: 1944, 1945
Signed xxxx Issued by Catholic Chaplain to the Forces: Patrick J. M. Kennh
Notes: LL B 117
Royal West African Frontier Force
Discharge Book:
Serial No.: D 135884
Regimental No.: NS/ 206856
Name: Peter Ntungwen
Enlisted at: Victoria on 9/1/43

Michael Nketi, *Njenka-Bali, 22 August 1988*

My name is Michael Nketi. This was the name I had when I was baptized. But when I was in the army the name I had was Mba Bawajn. I was born in 1910 at Bawajo. My father was called Bawajo while the name of my mother was Ndungteh. I was baptized at Soppo on 18 May 1926. I had left from Dschang when I was there and then went down to Soppo and got the baptism there. I was confirmed on 16 February 1936 at Mamfe. But before this I had my first Holy Communion at Soppo, a day after I was baptized on the 19 May 1926. Then I got married in the church at Kumboon on 26 October 1932 to Lucia Munika.

When I was still a child I used to move around the village playing from quarter to quarter. Also I used to go to the bush and tap palm wine. We also went cutting bamboo. As we played, sometimes, we even slept outside.

Then when I grew, I did some trading. We bought petty things from here and went and sold them at Abakwa (Bamenda), Bambui, and Bamessing. We used to buy fowls from there and brought here for sale.

I had also traveled to Calabar in 1942 when I had joined the army. How I managed to join the army was that, before I was taken to Calabar, an announcement was made that those who were interested to join the army could come. So I went to Bamenda and was taken.

Bafmeng

Rereading notes written in Bafmeng many years later was a reminder that many soldiers came from there, despite its isolation.

In 1988, after nine months in Bali-Nyonga, there was opportunity to travel to various mission stations and interview Cameroonians about their "life stories." One of the final stops was the mission of Bafmeng. It was a place to which I returned to stay for eight months from the end of 1988 till July 1989, and then again in 1991. The road from Bamenda to Fundong in Kom was fairly good in those days. However from Fundong to Bafmeng, a distance of 15 km was another matter. It was very difficult during the late rainy season and had many rough patches of broken culverts and deep mud. Entering what was known as Old Town, where the chief's palace was, the original Catholic mission church was on the left. Sundried blocks and rusted zinc were used for the church and the small meeting house nearby. Further on the main road, one came to "New Town," where there was a small Health Center, a large market, and a stone Catholic Church and presbytery. From the mid-1960s, the mission was also the home of Dominican Sisters from the Netherlands. After many years they had moved closer to Bamenda to a place called Bambui. The mission in 1988 was staffed by Fr. James Nielen and Brother Huub Welters, both Mill Hill Missionaries.

While I was in Bafmeng, there was a gathering of elders one evening in Old Town in the meeting house next to the church. The men sat along the walls of the sundried brick house. Lighting came from the small bush kerosene lamps that people placed on the dirt floor in front of them. They told their stories and answered questions. We took notes, made tape recordings, and snapped photographs. Among them were veterans of World War II.

Others were interviewed in the mission presbytery or at their own com-

58 *No Small Thing*

pounds. Some we met in the nearby village of Kuk, a place at the river on the road to Wum below the Bafmeng hills.

Peter Nji, *Kuk, Bafmeng, 20 November 1989*

My father was Mbeng and my mother Mbua. My mother delivered three male children. I was born in the German time. I helped in the farm and collected firewood. There was no school.

I went down to work on a plantation at Meselle, Victoria. It was a German farm of rubber and bananas. My brother Ignatius Gnai took me. I carried his things.

I also worked on the Mamfe Road bridge. A crocodile disturbed the work. People died. It was killed. At that time I was not married. After one or two years I came back,

I learned doctrine (*preparation for Baptism*) at Missele for two years. A Bakoko man was catechist. I came back to Kuk and went to Njinikom with Gabriel Fungeh for baptism by Fr. Jacobs.

(Baptism card: Peter Nchi [Nji] #5481 Njinikom; 1/11/36 Baptised; 2/11/36 First Com; 10/2/50 Conf [Wum LC 88]; married 17/2/47 Njinikom w. Veronica Mbong LB inf 360, LM 889; PIP 1955; 2nd Francisca Tigha, LB Wum 2794; 3/11/64 LM 210 Wum.)

The plantation was closed so I came back to Bamenda. Nigerian soldiers came to recruit for the army. Kuk people went: William Mbong, Vincent Toh, Michel Toh, Mbuh. We were sent to Victoria and then by ship to Lagos and on to Ghana. I remember Captain "Sibey." We had a chaplain but I do not remember his name. We spent two years with the Kru people before going to Cape Town and then Durban before crossing to India and Bombay. From there we went to Burma. I collected food etc. dropped by parachute.

Army No.: 38214, 8th G Regiment RWAFF

Private (?)

I sent money home for my brother for food. On discharge I received 15 pounds. When I returned I married Veronica. The dowry was 40 pounds; no brass rods (brass rods were a traditional form of currency used often as part of a dowry).

Michael Mom, *Kuk, 20 May 1989*

In addition to his interview he wrote a letter to Bafmeng on 25 October 1988. It is reproduced in the appendix. Michael described the medals he had received for service in India and Burma, two gold and two silver, including a gold Burma Star.

I was born at Kuk. The Germans had gone. My father was Ewai and my mother Ngia Sih. I grew and went to the plantations in 1930, at Mabetta. A

Wum man called Awa was headman. The pay was 3 pounds and 6 shillings per month. I did that for two years and then went to Makunange for one year.

I learned cook work at Soppo with Bishop Rogan and Fr. Roosendahl. Joseph Ojong, a Bayangi man, was the cook at Soppo. I was baptized at Bota by Fr. Jansen. My uncle worked a farm at Soppo and he took me to Soppo to learn cook work. I stayed for two years and six months.

In 1939 there was no work so I decided to go for soldier work before I will be a cook. I was given a rifle but was a cook. A father from Ghana was with us. I cooked throughout the war. An airplane brought food, steak, eggs, omelets. . . .

When I came back in 1946, I joined Fr. Akermann at Wum for two years and then with Nicholas Groot (see Bapt: Bota # 6319, 27/3/1938).

Later I went to Tiko and cooked for a white man at Tiko Airport mess, for twelve years at 30/ per mo.

Then I went to cook at Bota near the mission for two years; back to Limbe and the Basel Mission Bookshop for three years. Then to Kumba for the DO Mr. J. J. Bolman. My uncle died so I came home and stayed. I have twelve pickin.

He had a letter to the: Ambassador of France in Cameroon, 10 August 1977.
Particulars of service during 2nd WW.
Engagement: Bamenda
Date: 10 March 1941
81 Div (WA)
Private
Served: Bamenda, Gold Coast, Cape Town, Victoria, Ekeja, India, Lagos, Durban, Burma
Discharge: 31 March 1946; 5 years 22 days.
Conduct: Good; Fitness: A1
Campaign Stars etc
1939–45 Star; Burma Star, Defense Medal, War Medal 1939–45
Ex NA/38215

Michael Fong, Kuk, Bafmeng, 20 May 1989
I was born at Kuk to Bang and Kola.
(Bapt card: Bap: 1/1/39. 1st Com: 2/1/39
Confirmation: 1946 Alexandria, Egypt.
Married: Njinikom Elizabeth Tjia LM 915)
As a child at home I found firewood. When I grew I went to Buea and Missellele to work for the Germans clearing brush. I stayed with Musa Beng of Bafmeng for one year.

I joined the army at Victoria on 18 April 1942; 2442 Company; Private

We trained at Victoria and then went to Enugu for three months and on to Lagos for three months, to Freetown, Sierra Leone for three months before we entered a ship for Egypt. There were plenty ships. For two years I guarded prisoners. We had a leave of seven days for Jerusalem. I went to Bethlehem . "I ben walka all Jerusalem." At a house on a hill we saw the Red Sea far away. I bought pictures but they are all scattered.

Out of the army I went to the CDC for four years. And then back to country where I built houses.

Discharge: 30/9/46; 4 yrs 197 days.

From Lagos it was three days to Cameroon where they gave me five pounds

I took money from the army and sent it to Bamenda but my Pa "chopped all" (*used it all*).

James Ching, Bafmeng, 30 December, 1988

I was born at Chongtan, Su Bum. My father was Tasah and my mother Ni Nduk. I was a "guardian" for children in the compound. I did not go to school. *His father died and he went to the coast for five years.* I worked at Ndong, Kumba. I was not married. I was paid 15 shillings a month. As a head-man I was paid 2 pounds 5 shillings. I left the plantations and came home before I joined the army.

I joined the army at Santa in 1941. We trained at Victoria before taking a steamer to India. There was another man from here, Adamu Musa from Fonfuka, Bum. "We ben walka for soldier work. No ben go for look places." We went by motor to Burma. I was a runner in Co A, Battalion 8. "Cameroonian no ben de plenty." We "ben dig hole and sleep for ground."

I was never baptized and married Rebecca Mbu.

When we returned from India we went by steamer to Lagos and then Victoria. I took my uniform. We were given a book for work but I never showed the book and never went to look for work.

Discharge Book: Serial #D4400

Regimental No.: NA/138184

Ching Bum

Bamenda

Enlisted on 11/2/41

A very good and keen man. He has worked very hard at his job which has entailed sanitary duties.

I strongly recommend him to any prospective employer.

Ikeja, B S Meeredill, Maj.

1/3/46 81(WA) Div HQ, Coy (NA)

Particulars on discharge: Service 5 yrs 49 days of which 2 yrs, 193 days overseas.

Education: Sanitary and water duties course from 2-21 ? 7-45

Simple spoken English: yes
Literate in English: no
　　Hausa: no
Trade: laborer (plantation)

P 10 discharge: 31 March 1946
RWAFF Ord sec. 78(s)
Discharged from 81 (WA) Div, HQ Company
Age 35
5 ft 2 ½ in.
Ikedja, Records Officer, Nigeria Regt records.
Campaigns: 4th Burma
Medals: 1939–45 Star; Burma Star
NA 38114 Rank PtF, Ching Bum
Med cat on enlistment: FH
Payment on discharge: Cr bal: 41-3/
Leave pay: 1-6d pd day 4-4
Leave allow 11 d per day 2-11-4
War gratuity: 10-13-6
Overseas allow: 3-12-6
Plain clothes allow: 2

Mathias Tah, Bafmeng, 30 December 1988
I was born in Buh. My parents were Bai and Ekai. I never went to school but spent my time finding firewood.

In 1936 I went down to work on a plantation in Mabetta. At that time I had no wife.

I joined the army on 15 February 1941. We were in Victoria and Bota. I got my uniform and was training in 1941–42 in Ghana and then went to Lagos where we took a ship in 1943 to India and Burma and the war.

I was baptized in Ghana.

For 1944–45 we were in Burma and then returned to India and in 1946 went back to Lagos and Victoria.

After returning I was a bricklayer at Bamenda for two years. When the work finished I took "sawyer work." Then I stayed at Mbongkesu where I Married Sabina Fai from Buh. We had five children, three women and two men.

Martin Kuh, Bafmeng, 28 February 1989
My father was Njitoh and my mother was Njavuh. I was born at Ise before my father took me to Fungom. We were for inside dark and so I never went to school. I had three brothers. All died. My brother was a messenger at Komfutu.

I went with kola to Kano before I came back and joined the army at Victoria. I carried kola for a big man Peter Ncham—a Catholic. We carried his things.

At Victoria in 1942 I joined the army and they sent us for training in Enugu. There were plenty; many from Bafmeng. Then I went into a ship and went to Burma. We slept on the ship for about two months. We just went when war was almost finished. I just held a gun in my hand. Then we came back to Lagos. I just returned home and did my work as watchman at Buea and washed clothes. Then I came back to Bafmeng and worked coffee.

I used my money to marry Prudentia (she died). She had denied some man so I just backed her dowry to him.

I never had any children with my woman. That man who she denied bewitched her so she no go born. All the children are my brother's children.

Simon Rela, *Bafmeng, 21 September 1988*
I was born here during the English time. My father was Tefonyam and my mother was Gwanjam. All of them came from here.

I didn't attend school and I remained at home and was just working for my father. My mother had delivered just me alone. My mother wasn't a Christian.

I had worked in the Tiko banana plantation. I was staying in the camp. There were many people from Bafmeng here who were also there. I was the headman there and had twelve people under my control as was the rule. I had met those twelve people at Tiko. I worked there for two years and was paid 9/ as a headman. They used to give me food and fish every week. By then I didn't marry.

I had attended the church when I was in the army. I had left work on the plantation and came home here before joining the army. How I managed to join the army was that they had come to the palace and the chief took us and gave them to go and be soldiers.

We left from here, twelve of us, but when we reached only two of us were finally taken and the rest had to come back. Then we went to the Coast and stayed there for three months and from there we went to Ogoja in Nigeria. Then we took a ship and went to Egypt and it was there that I was baptized. We had met the father (*Chaplain Francis Woodman*) who baptized me, in Egypt. Later we reached Cairo and Jerusalem. At Egypt we were having training on how to go to war. There Germans were caught and we guarded them. We stayed there for two years. From Egypt we went to Jerusalem and when we returned we went to Cairo.

In Jerusalem we were taken to the church and then to Bethlehem.

There we were told how by the time when Jesus was born the king there had said that all baby boys should be killed and we were shown the heads which are there. In Jerusalem we saw blood at the place where Jesus was killed.

I knew Fr. Woodman. He was the one who gave a catechist to be teaching me doctrine in the camp, The man who taught was David and he was also the cook of the father. We were taught doctrine in English and I learned it for six months and was baptized at Kasserine in the camp of Fr. Woodman.

I came back here in 1946. They didn't give me plenty of money and as I came back I am working my farm.

I married my wife but didn't marry in the church till today. I got married to other women. My first wife died and now I am with Neh and she has been baptized. All my children had baptism. I only attend church "if that Sunday fine for me." But I don't go to the sacraments. As I returned I did nothing except farming. In the army I was taught just how to shoot a gun. I have six children and some are in the Coast and others are home here.

Catholic Soldiers Vade Mecum
Name: Simon Rela
Army No.: 16024
Home Mission: Njinikom

Status Anime	Date	Place	Minister
Baptism	1943	Kasserine	Fr. F. Woodman
Confirmation			
Easter Duty	1946	P 6 D	W. Ambrose
Matrimony			

Notes: On his own statement.
Issued by: Catholic Chaplain to the Forces

Gregory Che Yeh, Bafmeng, 21 September 1988

I was born here during the German time. My father was Chebe and my mother was Yeh. All of them were from here. My mother wasn't a Christian. As I grew I wasn't sent to school nor to the church and I stayed at home and fetched firewood for my father. Then I went to Buea in 1939 and was a laborer in the CDC plantation for a year and then I came back here. After that I went to the army. I was among those people who were taken from here in 1942 into the army. We had left from here to Bamenda then to Victoria, Calabar, and then to Lagos, where we took a ship to Egypt. We also went to South Africa, Cairo, and when we were given a leave, we went to Jerusalem. At Jerusalem I saw the church and went to Bethlehem. We had taken a train before going there and no father took us there. We stayed there for just six days.

Sextus Awa, Bafmeng, 30 December 1988

I was born in Mbongkesu. My parents were Peter Ndoh and Elizabeth Fuen. I was baptized by Fr. Jacobs at Njinikom in 1928. I received my baptism before my parents did. I never went to school but stayed at home.

In 1939 I went to the Coast to work on a plantation at Mbanda.

I joined the army at Bamenda. We were sent to Tiko for training and then to Victoria where we entered a ship for Calabar and then to "Nungo" and Kaduna, where we stayed for two months. After that we went to Lagos and took a ship to South Africa and on to Tobruk, where I spent one year. I visited Jerusalem with Fr. Woodman.

When I was discharged in 1946 I took 12 pounds and used it to marry my wife Aloysia Ndu. We had three children. I did work again for one year at Victoria, clearing.

Here are photographs of some of the interviewees
Photographs on pp. 64–68: © R. O'Neil, 1988

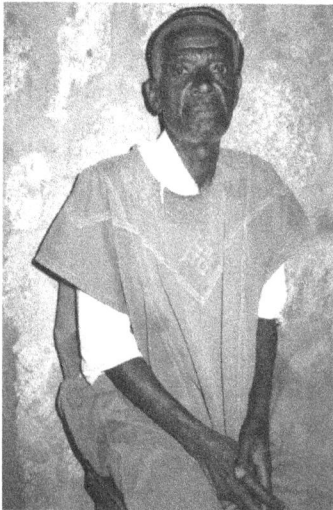

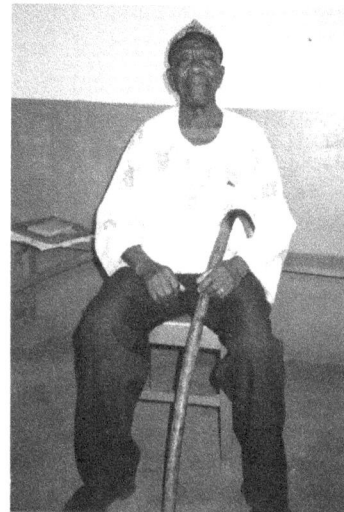

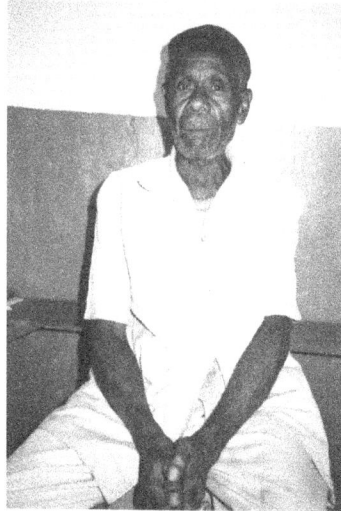

Old Town, Bafmeng

Sylvester, Catechist of Bafmeng, at
Lake Nyos, 1988

Bamenda and Other Places

Mr. Joseph Tepi Ndikum, Bamenda, 16 March 1984, and 14 July 2006

I was born in Babadjou on the French side (*in French Cameroun*) in 1918. My father was Ndikum and my mother Meintoh. She had four children; two died. I attended a Catholic Mission School at Babaju—on the French side. I was baptized at Mankon by Fr. Pierre Heymans in 1946. My papa moved and I ran to Nkongsamba in 1936. I had learned to be a blacksmith with my father. I had a knife and a gun. With Elias Nkweti I learned driving and took a three-ton Chevrolet—not a tipper—with salt from Nkongsamba to UAC in Bamenda. In 1940 I was driving in Bamenda and then in 1941, for six months from Bamenda to Mamfe, that is, through Widekum to Mamfe. Near Guzang at Tad there was one-way traffic, that is, up one day and down the next. There were accidents on the road and trees down. The Chevrolet was owned by Mathias Gwanella.

I was caught after Bali by soldiers with guns. They ordered me to leave the motor and pushed me inside their own motor. I slept at Bamenda for one night and then went to Victoria in a big motor. There I shaved and was thrown all the clothes (everything for skin). And then we went inside a steamer. We never saw Lagos but were two weeks at sea. We reached Sierra Leone. One morning we woke from sleep to see an airplane drop a bomb and it crashed. It was piloted by a woman who died. We came out and marched to Wilberforce Camp. We stayed until the dry season when we transferred to Porto Roco. It was far. The dry season came. . . . I had one month leave and returned to Bamenda. When I returned it was to Lagos.

In 1943 we entered a ship again. We never talked the name of the country. We were six weeks in the ship to Cape Town and Bombay. After three weeks we went by train to Madras for two months. In Madras I was the driver for a big man, General Woolner. We went to Calcutta. He inspected the place of the soldiers of the 4th Brigade. In the dry season we started walking.

We reached Burma. There was no food. We were near the war place. At "Cox's Bazar" airplanes dropped the food. We attacked. My hand was shot and I lost my index finger in the fight. I remained in India for one year. The English said to go back home. We were put in a ship and went though the Suez Canal, to Egypt, Malta, and Lagos. That was in 1946.

I could either remain in the army or go for country. I kept money with General Woolner. I took a paper and claimed the money here in Bamenda. With it I bought my present house. I wasn't married. I drove a motor from Mamfe to Douala to take cement for the PWD.

I also worked for a European woman with the Education Department, Domestic Science. I was a driver for her in Nso.

I never worked for the government again. I took my money to buy a three-ton Bedford and began to carry cargo for the Catholic mission, Bamenda, from Victoria.

I took other money and with Mission support bought another Chevrolet. Then I married for Church. My house was already built and I bought a second.

I started carrying for Fr. Leo Onderwater at Bambui Mission to Nso, Nkar, and Okoyong; not only Victoria.

Mr. Ndikum *(continued on 14 July 2006)*

The war with Japanese was "no small thing." Many people died. Sometimes we walked on blood.

In 1945 the war finished. Any soldier who wanted could go back home. Others were given chance to be soldiers in peace time. I said "I de go country." After all the mines were moved we entered ships and went through the Suez Canal back to Bota. The army left us with all our equipment. I only took a gas mask. In Sierra Leone I put my money, 200 pounds, in Barclays Bank and transferred it to Victoria. With the money I bought a Bedford lorry in Cameroon.

The late Archbishop Paul Verdzekov told the story of J.T. Ndikum collecting the students at Enugu Seminary in Nigeria and bringing them home over the Mamfe Bamenda Road in his Bedford. But that was long after his service in Burma [July 18, 2006].

Misseng Ngong, *Bafmeng, 21 September 1988*

I was born here and I am 60 years old now. My father was Ngong Meh. When I was a small child, I never attended school. My father wasn't a Christian. I didn't attend doctrine. When I grew I only was a trader and went to Nigeria to sell kola nuts at Ebi. I had joined the army when I was 15 years old. I had joined the army because when I went to Nigeria in 1940 I had seen one ex-soldier in the market and was determined to go to the army. Then they came and told the chief that they wanted people to go to the army and when they were choosing people I stood here and was taken. When we were taken we went first to Victoria. From there we went to "Mokudange." We stayed there for about one year and were sent overseas.... I was there with Abantu, who was from here. We had so many captains because there were many battalions too. There was one called Major Box and another was Captain Messing.

When I returned from Gambia to Enugu, we were given a leave and I joined with one European to go to Yaoundé to leave people who were going on leave.

We also went to the Middle East and Cape Town and stayed there for three months. We used to move by ship. We also went to Tripoli in Libya. There we were guarding prisoners. I also went to Jerusalem with our company on leave. I wasn't baptized there.

Fathers used to come there, and the day I was to be baptized I was sent on guard. I came back here in 1946. On return I was given just a small amount of money. As I came back I began farming. In the army I was a corporal.

I came back before I married my wives and their names are Senifa, Mbong-hafa, Tetoghe, and Jeh. I have fifteen children. Only that wife who died used to attend the Catholic Church. My children were baptized in the Catholic Church.

One of my children is at Limbe, another is working at Douala, and one is at Bamenda. When I was in Gambia we used to go to the bush only. If somebody did a bad thing he was put in prison for forty-two days.

Particulars of Service (document)

Misseng Ngong

During the Second World War, 1939–1945

Place of engagement in the army: Victoria

Date: 19/3/42

Company/battalion: 4th Battalion

Rank/grade: Lance Corporal

Places Served during the War: Victoria, Gambia, Sierra Leone, Gold Coast, Middle East, Alexandria, Tripoli, Benghazi

Date of discharge: 31/12/46

Cause of discharge: On demobilization

Period served in the army: 4 years 90 days

Conduct on discharge from the army: Good

Jacob Jaff, Kisong, 14 September 1988

When I left Bali I went and was catechist at Ndu for two years. After Ndu I went and made one year at Jakiri and from there I went to the army. By that time they used to catch us by force to join the army. (They had told the Fon of Nso to give people for the army and we were given.) They came and caught us from Kumbo when I had gone there for the market. Then we went to Bamenda and stayed for three months. From there we passed through Victoria to Lagos and it was there that I signed my name in the army in 1940. We were sent to the Middle East. We took a ship and went to Cape Town in South Africa. Then we also went to Cairo, Alexandria, Tripoli, and Benghazi. There we learned how to fire a gun. I never killed anybody there. I only used to guard prisoners. I was with Jacob Fuli, Sam Kwanje of Tatum, Jacob of Ngong. We had also gone to Jerusalem with Fr. Woodman. He used to move with us and looked out for all the soldiers. When we were to leave the work they took us to Lagos where we signed a book of discharge and then we were brought to Victoria and then we came to Bamenda.... They were to give us money but till today we haven't seen it. When I returned I hadn't anything nor any trade. (Many who came back from the army had nothing. I don't receive even a pension.)

Jacob Jaff, Kishong, September 1988.
Photo: © O'Neil

I was given an African medal. Major Breeyah was our officer. He was at one time the District Officer (DO) of Buea. He was the one who took us to all those places. Paul Mimba was an army man who was with me, and he was a white man.

There was no black who at that time was a captain but there were many sergeants.

We had a certain meeting when we came back here called the "Fraternal Union of Old Soldiers."

There was no pastor in the army, but Fr. Woodman used to cater for all soldiers. I never saw him again.

Mr. Jaff was not a Catholic but a member of the Basel Mission.

Agug John Ngwa, *Guzang, Moghamo, 5 August 1988*
Mr. Ngwa did not join the army but was employed building an airport near Mamfe.

Boys and girls who passed the Standard 6 exams were not employed. So at the end of that year my appointment was terminated. That was in 1939. So I had to go home. I had nothing doing. I thought I could do something. My father said I should go to the South. I went down to Mamfe in 1940. That was during the Second World War. In 1940 there was construction of the Besonabang airport. I went there and was employed as an assistant time-keeper. I worked there until the airport was completed and the first plane landed. Then we closed up and came back home. I had nothing doing. I went back again to Bamenda to look for a job. I tried my hand at a number of things and I didn't succeed, but actually I succeeded in getting a job with the Native Authority (NA), now known as the Council, and I was posted to Bali NA school now Bali Council School where I taught for some years and then passed the entrance examination to teacher training. That was in 1945 and I went to Kumba Teacher Training College.

Clement Ngu Ngwa, Bafut Mission, 20 February 1989
He was born in 1907 in old Nta Chu. His father was Ngwa and his mother Ngum; she was given "trouble baptism" and named Veronica. His brother was a Basel Mission pastor, Suh Ambe. Bafut is about 16 miles from Bamenda.

At ten years I went to a white man as a "kitchen boy." That was in about 1920. He was a soldier named Captain "Boucher." Then I was for five years with DO "Oxworth" as a steward. In 1928 I went to work on a German plantation as a motor mechanic and blacksmith. I spent 5 years 10 months in the Bota workshop. In 1939 because of the war there was no work so I went back to country and worked for the Bafut chief, Acherebi II. In 1940 I showed the DO my certificate and went to soldier work in 1941. We trained at Bota and then went to Sierra Leone for two years and then India and Burma. I was in the 4th Battalion, a corporal. (*A captain signed his card: "mechanic work: fine," in 1946. His pay was 3/6d*).

After the war he worked with "custodial property for two years." "Not paid fine: 2/6d" I wrote to the army labor office in Enugu; never paid me. I did a refresher course in Nigeria for one year as a mechanic. I came out as a Grade 1 motor mechanic. There was no work.

Document: Clement Ngwa: Enlisted 14/3/1941
Nigeria Regiment RWAF Force
Certificate of Service
Military condition: exemplary
Discharge 30 June 1945 Corporal
RWAFF
4 years 109 days
Age: 39 years

English profession: blacksmith/ driver
Badge: 4th Burma
Refresher course: Enugu 1 October 1948–7 May 1949.

Thomas Go-oh Natang, *Bodji, Kom, 20 September 1988*
Thomas was born in Malenda, Bakossi. He had been brought to Njinikom to care for the child as a "nurse baby," of Edward Ntangte. In Njinikom he studied the catechism for two years in preparation for baptism. He then worked in the mission as a servant in the house, helping the cook and another man who did the cleaning. While there he worked for Fr. Thomas Burke Kennedy and Fr. Bill Boetskes. It was Fr. Woodman who called him to be his steward and orderly in the army. He continued to work for Fr. Woodman after the War and to the end of his life in Cameroon. Fr. Woodman is buried in Njinikom Mission.

Thomas Go-oh, Bodji, Kom, 23
September 1988.
Photo: © O'Neil

A telegram came from Fr. Woodman to Tom at Mukuru "Tom, come for army."
I received a uniform and a gun but only served as a steward to Father. We went to Lagos where after five days we joined a steamer for three weeks to Cape

Town where we spent three nights. Then we took four weeks again through the Red Sea to Cairo and Kasserine. I remember others: Alois Suh, Nkain, Mudake, Sufala, Anthony Tio. Father Woodman was a captain. He made Mass, heard confessions, and baptized. He was chaplain of the number 1 group. One big group with officers filled a ship. We guarded captured soldiers. They wore white uniforms with black. We gave them chop and they helped with work. We were in Tobruk for six months, Tripoli for six months, and Dana for seven months. We went to Benghazi. I traveled with Father to see soldiers where they lived. When the war finished we were in Alexandria. Once we went to Jerusalem for seven days. It was me, Father's driver, and Fr. Woodman.

With Fr. Woodman I walked. We went to Bethlehem and saw a small door, exactly like my house. Outside the church was not fine but inside, we entered for heaven.

When I returned on my first trip from Nigeria I returned married (LM 836 Njinikom, 22/4/1946, Elizabeth, LB 29/5/27 Njinikom; born 17/5/27).

Thomas was at home in Njinikom for one year after the war. Fr. Woodman was back from the army and working in another mission, Basseng. He called Tom to continue as a steward there.

After one year I had a telegram from Fr. Woodman, "Come to Basseng." . . . Father used to join old soldiers.

On leaving army: Nigeria PO Savings Bank, Accounts Branch 126466: paid 26-12/-5d
Discharge: 28 February 1946
Ikedja
Records Office
Nigeria Regiment Records
93 Group
Headquarters Pioneer Corps
"With colour": 3 years 1 day
Age 25, hgt: 5'7½"
Bamenda tribal marks on face, multiple scars on legs.
Private NA 11761
Medals: North Africa; Africa Star; Defense

Pa Che Tamankag, Old Town Mankon, Bamenda, 2 August 1989
My name is Che Tamankag. I was born in 1916 at Mankon, Bamenda. My father was Tamankag and my mother was called Fei. They were all Mankon people. They were all farmers.

When I was a child of about seven years, I used to do farming with my parents. I used to carry corn from the farm to the house. I also fetched firewood for my parents.

Then I left and became a laborer. I carried the cargo of the District Officer (DO) at Bamenda and went to the bush when he went out station. We used to go to Nso, Nkambe, and Wum.

After this I went to tap rubber with the Germans. We were there with one Endeley. We also established a raffia palm bush there. I was paid three pennies. Those who were highly paid received six pennies.

Then in 1930 I went to Nigeria to work and it was there that I joined the cook work with one white man called Haoness. I was there till 1939 that the war broke out. Because of the war the white man left and went back to England as he was British. Then he said that he never knew whether he was to come back again. Because that white man left and I had no work I had to join the army as a cook. We stayed at Ogoja then headquarters at Enugu. I had joined the army in 1941. From Ogoja we went to Lagos, Ibaden, and then left to Burma. There our captain was Major Walman. There were two chaplains with us, one for the Catholics and the other for the Presbyterians. But I didn't know them. In the army I was paid one shilling a day, that is, per month I received 1 pound 10 shillings. At the army I registered like a man from British Cameroons as Cameroon was by then called. We had passed through the Gold Coast, Gambia, and took troopships to Burma. According to war method one was to defend himself, people died but I killed nobody.

From Burma we went back to Lagos, passed to Victoria (now Limbe), then through Mendeck because there was no road in West Cameroon and came to Bamenda. We were moving by night and upon dawn we went to the DO in the morning.

There were many of us from the British Cameroons in the army there but I can't remember them again. When I joined the army in Lagos I was considered a Nigerian until Burma where I said I was from the British Cameroons.

At Bamenda DO Keh came and gave us the ex-servicemen cards and we were promised employment but since then no work was given to me.

Because they gave me no work, I had to join cook work again. This time with a certain Mr. Ngip a custom officer at Santa. I worked with him for only six months.

From there I went to Lagos to work with a DO there as cook. I worked with him for one year and then left back to Bamenda, where I was working with one Mr. Sandal. He took me and we went to Ibaden. He was a Forest Assistant. We were together until he left for his country and I then came back to Bamenda and joined the Catholic rest house as cook. I had stayed with that Forest Assistant at Ibaden for one year six months.

When I left the Catholic rest house I was taken after the Plebiscite period (in 1961 voters in the British Southern Cameroons chose to unite with French Cameroun at independence. The Plebiscite was organized by the United

Nations) because they saw my ex-servicemen card to work as a cook in the camp. They had also seen my Discharge Book. I was paid at the camp one shilling a day.

After this the council at Bamenda (i.e., Municipal Council) took me and I became the head watchman in the market. It was from there that I retired and I'm staying at home like this.

Before I went to the army I was married to one wife already and on return I got married to two others. I had three wives but one died and I am now living with two. I have sixteen children. One of them went right to the USA and came back and is now in Yaoundé; and some are still attending school. I was never baptized.

(Excerpts from some documents)

Nigeria form Res 11

Part I

Ex Service Introduction Card, Date 14/9/1946

Rank : Spr.

Army trade: Book Gp B Class II

Royal West African Frontier Force Discharge Card: Trade on joining the army: Steward Boy

Present army trade and classification therein: European Book, Gp B class II-10/3/46

Certificate of Discharge:

Name: Che Tamankag

Date: 30 September 1946

Cause of discharge: On demobilization

Discharge under Sec. RWAFF ord. Sec,78

Unit from which discharged: N Section Signals 82 (WA) Division.

With colours: 5 years 47 days

Age: 35 Height 5 ft 2 in.

Marks and scars: nil

Place: Ikeja

Signature and rank, xxxxxx Records Officer, Nigeria Regiment Records.

Medal Awards:

Clasps 1, 1939-1945, Star

Mention in dispatches: any special act of gallantry or distinguished conduct brought to the notice in superior orders: 1 at Burma-Star

War Medal: 1: 2 ? (25/4/59, V B Grunga, City Council Stamped and signed)

Peter Che Mama, Old Town, Mankon, Bamenda, 12 August 1989

I was born in 1927 at Mankon, Bamenda. I had army number 11960. My father was Musa Ndefu and my mother was Mankah Sirri. They were all farmers and all of them came from Mankon here.

When I was a small child, we used to tap palm wine. I had wanted to be sent to school but was not sent because my parents never knew the value of education. The wine we tapped we drank in the house and some of it was sold. Also I used to fetch firewood for my parents.

Then it was 1942 that I heard that they were recruiting army officers at Bamenda Up-Station. I left and went there and they examined me and I was taken into the army.

From the station in Bamenda we were taken to Limbe. We stayed there for three months and it was there that uniforms were given to us. Then we left to Lagos and were there until Christmas. We also stayed at Ikeja.

Then on 1 January 1943 we took a ship to Egypt. We took three months to reach Egypt. There we were taken to the battlefield. The field tents were built and the uniform was changed. Then we also went to Italy and there some Italians were caught and taken to Benghazi. There they were put inside a fence and we were the people who were guarding them. There we also used to unload war equipment from the ship. We stayed at Benghazi for two years only guarding those prisoners.

Then in 1946 we were changed and sent to Egypt. We stayed for two months and then we left for Alexandria. When there the United Nations sent a message by radio that we were to go back the following day. Then we packed everything of ours and at one o'clock we left to go and enter the ship and from there we returned and reached Calabar. Then finally we arrived at Lagos from where we were taken to Victoria (Limbe). While at Lagos we had been given leave to reach and take our pay back here in Cameroon. During the war, we were given just a small amount of about 1 pound and 50 shillings and that our pay shall actually be given after the war.

Our chaplain was Fr. Woodman. He had been at Mankon here and left from here with us to the war. We had many captains. There was one Bricket, Blei, and also Benedict, who were there as captains with us. As we were told to reach here and take our pay, till date, nothing has been given to us here. Even at Bamenda Station the DO had told us that they were to reengage us. There after nothing again was said to us and even the pension they said was to be paid to us has never since then been paid.

Since I left the army I never went out to work anything again. I have been at home working coffee and tapping palm wine. I also cultivate yams. It is from all these that I am managing life now.

I got married to Theresa Mankaah in 1948 when I had returned from the army. I had ten children with her but one died and there are nine who are living. Some of these children are attending secondary school, others are already married and some are traders.

When we were in the army each church had its own chaplain there and I used to attend the Presbyterian church (*Basel Mission*). We had gone to Jerusalem and had been given holy water if they knew you were a Christian. Then we also went to Bethlehem and were shown where Jesus was born. We were also sold Bibles. We were there for four days. One was not forced to go there. There were two options. Either to go to Cairo or to Bethlehem. I was lucky and my name fell that I should go to Jerusalem.

Pa Lucas Fru, *Old Town Bamenda, 12 August 1989*

I was born in 1923 at Mankon, Bamenda. I had the army number 11819. My father was Wanki and my mother was Ngum. They were all from Mankon here and they all did farming.

When I was young I used to follow my parents to the farm. Also I did fetch firewood for them. Then when I grew I was searching for a job in town and had seen some soldiers who were on leave. They asked me to go to Bamenda Up-station and see the white man who was there. When I reached there he examined me and gave me books and told us that we were to leave immediately. He had given us food money. We were forty-five of us who left at that time. Some of them were Ndifor and Muma from Bagangu. Then the following day we were taken to Victoria. We were there for two weeks. Then a ship came and took us to Calabar and we were there for three months. From Calabar we left for Lagos. From there we went to South Africa. Then we went to the battlefield. I didn't kill anybody but my friends had killed some of our enemies. When a person was killed he would just be left in the bush to get rotten there. We had also gone to Dakar. I had stayed three years two months at the war. Father Keke was our chaplain and our captain was Mr. Hans.

From Lagos we reached Limbe where we were discharged. Then we arrived in Bamenda. At Bamenda the DO asked us to wait and that our pay would be given but till date nothing has been given nor the work they had promised to give us.

I never attended school. I got married when I had returned from the army to Maria Manka'ah. My father was the one who arranged everything about that marriage. He wouldn't have forced her to me should I have refused to take her.

I have eleven children. Some are in Kribi and Muyuka. And some are learning work as mechanics and carpenters. The one who is staying now with me is already married.

I manage my life now from the retail trade I am making and also from the palm wine just in Bamenda here and the retail trade is also done just here.

Pa Charles Atanga Moma, *Akum, 3 August 1989*

My father was called Moma and my mother was Lum. They were all from Akum here. All of them were Christians. They were baptized at Akum. I was born at Akum here on the 24 December 1920.

When I was a small child I did a bit of trading in the selling of small things like salt. We used to buy the salt from Babadjou. After that I went to the coast with my friend David Akor. There I lived with him.

I first started staying at Victoria and was looking for work. Then I began to work in the sea. We used to load the ship in John Holt (*a trading company*). I was paid 1 shilling 6 pence a day.

After that work I came home. We were many of us from Bamenda there. The cook was a Bamenda man and the assistant cashier was a Bamenda man.

When I came here I joined the army because I had liked to serve in the British Empire. Then we left from here and went to Calabar. We were at Calabar for two years and during this time the war was going on. Then again we left to Kano. From Kano we went to Lagos. From Lagos we went to Mendipo. Later we left for overseas. As we were going the war was so serious and we were in the ocean for three months. Our ship pilot came and directed us to pass through the Suez Canal. We came to a bay in the Suez Canal, and another ship came and took us. . . . Then one night orders came that we should go to Benghazi and we went there.

There, so many groups of doctors came and tested and examined us and in the night the whole lot of us were taken and questioned why I joined the force and my reply was, I joined the force to serve the British Empire. People were picked from many groups and we were about 600 who formed a battalion. Then we were going to where we didn't know, and the following day we were in India. We started touring and were with both blacks and whites.

My first place I know was Burma. There the war was serious. We were there for eleven months. One could not put a light during the night for fear of attack. We only used small stoves to prepare food. Until the war ended some people lost their lives.

We only counted people when we came together. Some people lost their eyes and others their hands. We were called and told we were going home. Then we entered a ship and dropped at Victoria Port in the British Cameroons. Everyone had to find out his way back to his home. That was in October 1946.

I was at home for some time doing nothing and I found things hard. I then went back to Limbe to work in the sea. We used to paint the ships and also load cargo.

In the army we were given pocket allowances and we had free food. Our captain was Captain Bottle. The father who was with us was Fr. William. The fathers used to visit the camps weekly for Mass. I can remember Fr. William because he liked me so much. He was a captain.

At Limbe we started as ex-servicemen and I was paid two shillings a day. I was there for thirty-five years. From Limbe I left and came here. There were many people from Bamenda side at Limbe with me. I had got married by that time. When I was at Limbe I married Marceline Shiri. I had five children but one died. Some of them are at the coast and others are in Bamenda-town.

I was baptized while at war. This was at Burma. I cannot remember the name of the priest who baptized me. I had been shot in the back during the war and that is why I have this scar on my back. When I was shot in the back and became sick it was then that I was given baptism and so I can't know the father who gave me Baptism.

I manage to sustain my life now on the pension that I receive. I also do some farming now.

Before I got married I had come from Limbe and was shown the girl I wanted to marry. I saw her and she was all right for me and I got married to her. I had gone back to Limbe and after all the native celebrations were made my brothers brought her down to me. I didn't attend school.

Excerpts from some of his documents.

Royal West African Frontier Force

Discharge Book

Serial No.: N4580

Regiment No.: AN/16338

Lang Moma

Enlisted at Bamenda Date: 5/10/42

Final assessment of conduct and character on leaving the colours: Military conduct: Exemplary.

Testimonial: Duties with zeal and efficiency.

Place : Lagos; Signature or rank (Major commanding) African Details Camp.

Date: 28/2/1946

Trade on joining the army: Trader

Present army trade and classification: Nil

Any additional trade in which classified while serving: Nil

Certificate of Discharge: Date: 9 March 1946

Cause of Discharge: RWAFF Ord. Sec 78(A) Medically unfit for military service,

Unit from which discharged: African Details Camp.

Service on date of discharged with colours: 3 yrs, 156 days.

Description of soldier on discharge: Age: 22. Height 5 ft 0 ins.

Place: Lagos; Signature (Records Officer) Nigeria Regiment Records

Pius Che Tafor, Akum, 9 August 1989

My father was Tafor and my mother was Shirri Mafor. They were all from Akum and all of them farmers.

When I was a small child I was with my father and was working with him in the compound, because I did not attend any school. Then when I grew and was about 18 years I went and joined the army. This was in 1940.

By 1939/40 the army camp had been at Santa and also at Mile 4. I had joined the army with those at Mile 12. I had joined the army because I was looking for money and also because when they used to march it was nice and I was interested in the whole thing. We were many of us who had joined the army and included were Benjamin Asongwe, Peter Fomukong, James Ngoh, and David Akor. From where we joined the army (i.e., Mile 12), we were sent for training on how to shoot and fight, and after they saw some of us who were young and sent us to the school of Infantry and Education at Zaria to be trained on how to read and write. At the school we were taught infantry fighting and it had acted as an adult school because we had joined the army as illiterates. I had obtained a stage II certificate of education from that school.

After the training we were sent overseas. The war had started from 1939 to 1945 when it ended and in 1946 we returned back home. I can't remember our chaplain but I was baptized while in the Nigerian army years later in Ibadan. (His baptism card noted he was baptized by Rev. Fr. A. Jennings on 3 August 1958; No. 2156.)

When we were at Accra, some of my friends had betrayed me and I was discharged without the knowledge of our commander who was on leave, I returned and stayed in the house for about six months, and then the commander returned and saw me in town in civilian dressing, he asked me what was wrong and I explained to him that I never knew anything and he ordered me to return to the camp. My commanding chaplain was Major Dolf and the battalion officer was Lt. Wilson.

I had left from there and come back home and stayed here just for three months. And in 1947 I went again to Nigeria and joined the army at Enugu. I had decided to go back to Nigeria by myself. Nobody asked me to do so. When I reached there I was given no training because they saw that I had been in the army, I had maintained my rank and everything. Then I stayed there for eighteen years and it was from there that I was given this Discharge Book; and during the Plebescite in 1961 I came and joined the Cameroon army.

From Nigeria I came here and was sent to Ngoundere to learn French and to be taught how to do commanding in French. While in Nigeria I was paid 1:10/ at the start and then when I became a corporal I was now paid at 2:10/. In Nigeria we stayed at the camp and there was one battalion for each region.

In Cameroon I had worked first in Bamenda then at Bangante and then lastly at Bafoussam. In was from Bafoussam that I retired in 1969.

I had got married in 1948 at Akum here to Charista Lum. I had made all the marriage arrangements by myself. After she died I got married to another. I have a total of thirteen children. The first of the children have completed school and are outside doing their own businesses. Presently I manage to live by the pensions which I receive from Nigeria and Cameroon. Nigerian government is still giving me a pension as ex-service soldier from there. Two years have passed that they haven't paid me, but my pension from the Cameroon government is all right. While I was in the army in Nigeria they knew that I was a Cameroonian.

We had suffered in the army fighting in the bush with Japanese. About food—a plane used to come and give us food in the forest. As regards our pay they gave us just a small thing and we were promised our pay when the war was to end and till today nothing has been paid to us.

Excerpts from some documents that include service in the RWAFF during World War II and later the Nigerian Army.

Nigeria Military Forces NMF/Form/34

Certificate of service: Serial No.: 40454; Regt No.: 205983

Name: Pius Che Tafo

Enlisted at Enugu on 21/3/1949

Military Conduct: Exemplary; Testimonial: Service in the military for 18 years and is a very good type of soldier; Place: Ibaden: Date: 16/4/61; Signature: Officer Commanding

Certificate of Discharge: Date: 13/11/1961; Rank: Corporal; Cause: Completion of service, to Pension

On Discharge Unit: 4 QONR;

Service: With colours: 12 yrs 7 months 20 days; 1st previous Service: 3 yrs, 8 mths, 20 days (RWAFF); 2nd Previous service: 1 yr 9 mths 17 days. Total 18 years 2 months 1 day.

Description of soldier on discharge: Age: 34; height 5 ft 11 inches.

Tribal marks: scars or peculiarities likely to assist identification: Slight mark under eyes. Place: Lagos, 29 September 1961; Signature: Officer in Charge of Pays and Records: NMF

Trade on enlistment: Labourer

Distinguished conduct: 1939–1945; War Medal; and Independence Medal; Congo Medal.

Gastong Nwaneghe, Bessom, Moghamo, 20 August 1989

My father was Awoh and my mother was Eboyen. They used to do farming, that is, tapping palm wine and cutting palm nuts. And all of them, or rather my mother, was a girl from Enyoh while my father was from Bessom here.

When I was a small child by then I knew nothing; then when I grew I went down to Kumba. I had gone there just alone and there I was at Fiango with David Akwanang. I did trading while at Kumba. We used to trade in pigs to Victoria. One pig was sold for 2 to 3 pounds. I did this for about five years that I was at Kumba.

From there it was when the war had come I stood one day at the door and soon saw soldiers passing from Bamenda to Victoria, I became interested and then went and also wrote my name to join the army. This was in 1942. My army number was 16366. The David Akwanang with whom I was at Kumba never even knew that I was intending to join the army. I had liked to join the army and David never knew that I was going to go there. By the time we were accepted we were given one penny each as food money and were ordered to go to Victoria to join the army. While in Victoria a medical doctor examined us and a uniform was given and we went to Esonge, where our camp was . From Esonge we went to Lagos at Ikeja. There we fought with the town people and the next day we entered the ship and had stayed inside the sea for two months and reached Egypt. There at Egypt we started work and took leave and went to Jerusalem.

In 1945 the war ended and in 1946 we were discharged to go back to Africa. Then we entered the ship and went to Esonge, where they were calling us Satan people because we liked to fight. Then a vehicle came and took us to Bamenda. At Bamenda the DO asked us to go to our villages and said he was to employ us but after no work was given.

By the time we were at the war I had shot a person, the enemy. There were some priests and they were the people who gave us Communion. There was only one chaplain with us in the war.

I was paid about 1 pound 10 shillings per month as my salary. We were paid each month.

I had also reached Burma. Some people remained there because by the time the war ended and we were returning, widows came crying for us to stay there and marry, and some soldiers remained there to get married to those women. I have forgotten the name of our captain.

I had returned and got married here. When the DO did not give us work I began to do farming. It was from that farming that I obtained money to be able to get married.

At war they used to feed us with rice and there was enough meat.

I had attended no school before going to the army. I had attended only the vernacular school. They didn't take into consideration the vernacular school I had attended before taking me to the army. At war they never allowed us to have any contact with women.

By the time we were at war we used to dig trenches and would be shooting war-bombers from there. We used to stay inside those trenches. It was a plane that used to come and supply us with food. We used to bury those of our soldiers who were killed. Burial was done by caterpillars. They used to indicate the number of soldiers that were killed so as to know how to reinforce the forces.

Jabuke Mbafor, *Ashong, Moghamo, 21 August 1989*

My father was Mbafor and my mother was Eken. They were all people from Ashong here and they did farming throughout their lives.

By the time I was a small child I used to carry fowls to the farm with my parents (and) used to clear farms for my parents. Later on I did marketing and went as far as Widekum (*on the Mamfe–Bamenda Road*) from where I bought palm oil. I also went to Mbembe, Mesaje and also Dschang from where I used to buy salt and brought it here for sale.

Then in 1942 I had joined the army. I had told my father that I would join the army. By then my father had been imprisoned in Bamenda because they said he had embezzled tax money. When I had reached Bamenda I was taken as a soldier.

From Bamenda we went through Nkongsamba down to Victoria and then through the sea to Kano. We were there for two months and from there we went to Lagos.

We used to be in the army with white women who were also soldiers. I had been given a medal by one of them. From Lagos we went to Cape Town. We also went overseas for the war. Then too we were at Egypt. We had war chaplains. There was one for the Catholics and one for the Presbyterians. We used to work including Sundays.

I had worked in the army for three years and had been given a Defense Medal and War Medal 1939–1945. There they used to pay us after five days. By this time we were returning, we passed through the sea and were there for two weeks and then left from there to Victoria in Cameroon. Then we left from Victoria and reached the DO in Bamenda. At Bamenda the DO told us to preserve all our documents and that we shall be called up when there is work. Then by the time I was called to come and start work again I had refused because I was now involved in women and had already got married. Before I went to the farm I had already got married to one girl from Bali. Later she died. I had arranged everything by myself.

I manage to live now from the coffee and kola nuts which I planted on return from the army in 1946.

I had eight children but three of them died. And the remaining five are just at home here with me.

Excerpts from Documents:
Royal West African Frontier Force Discharge Book
Serial No.: D/44843; Regiment No.: NA 206875; Name: Jabuke Mbafo
Enlisted at Victoria on 7 January 1943
Military Conduct: Good
Testimonial: A soldier who has worked well. He is very clean and sober.
Place: Ikeja; Date: 7/6/46
Service: 3 years 173 days of which 2 years, 25 days overseas.
Trade on joining the army: Farmer; Signature XXX CC Unit
Certificate of Discharge
Date 30 June 1946; Rank: PTE
Cause of Discharge: On Demobilization; RWAFF Ord. Sec. 78(5)

Unit from which discharged: 2424 Company (WA), Army Pioneer Corps
Service on date of discharge: 3 years, 173 days.
Description of soldier on discharge: Age 27 yrs; Height 4 ft 10 in.(?); Place
    Ikeja
Signature: XXX Records Officer, Nigerian Regt. Records
Payment on discharge: 18 pounds 18 shillings 6 pence

Wilfred Mba, *Enyoh, Moghamo, 20 August 1989*

My army number was LN2555. My father was Mbacheu and my mother was
Elizabeth Abeck. They were all from Enyoh here. My mother was a housewife
while my father was a preacher in the Presbyterian Church. He had started
working here at Enyoh and then for the whole of Moghamo and later was sent
to Bafoucho.

I was born in 1924 at Enyoh. Because my father was a preacher he had sent
me to go and attend the Mbengwi Presbyterian School in 1936. They used to
teach in the English language and the H/M there by then was Hon. S. T. Muna.
I had also attended the vernacular school at Bafoucho before leaving to
Mbengwi. At the Mbengwi school the school manager was one Mr. Emanuel,
and some mates there included Isaac Anoma, who was a boy from Bafoucho,
and Christopher Tasi from Metta. In that school they used to teach all the subjects that are being taught in schools now: e.g., History, Hygiene, Arithmetic,
English, etc. Before one could ever go to the English school an exam was written
and unless one passed that exam he wouldn't go there.

At the school in Mbengwi in the morning we stood on the line and would
march in an open room and then the children would go to their various classes
and would be there studying till closing time. Some teachers in the school at
Mbengwi included Mr. S. T. Muna from Metta, Mr. Bai from Bayange, Mr.
Tambi from Enyoh and Mr. Essi from Metta, and even late J. G. Nkangsen (*he
became Moderator of the Presbyterian/Basel Mission Church*). I had attended
that school for five years and had competed Standard 5.

From that school I left and joined the army on 5 March 1942. I had joined
the army because by the time we were at Bafoucho I saw one beautiful girl and
had desired to marry her but had no money and I thought that by joining the
army I would be able to have money to marry her. I had gone to Bamenda three
times to be recruited into the army but was refused because they said that I was
too small. Then the last time I persisted and was crying to be admitted and at
last they accepted to take me. This was at Bamenda. We were together there
with Jeremiah Mbafor from Ashong.

From Bamenda we went down to Victoria and it was there that we had our
training. When they later on realized that I had completed Standard 5 I was
taken and put to be the secretary inside the office. At Gambia we built roads
preparing to attack the Germans who were already at Dakar. This was in 1942.

As we were preparing to attack the Germans it happened that the Germans surrendered unconditionally not to fight again, and we had to return to Gambia. We had returned and stayed at Yundum Aerodrome (*now Banjul International Airport*). It was then that I entered a plane for my first time. We had left Gambia to Cape Town and while there I was selected to go to the 55th Army General Hospital Gambia to be trained as an army nurse. After training I was then working as an army nurse under Grade 3. We had left Gambia to Sierra Leone and were there for two weeks; and from there we went back to Lagos and while there we were given a leave of sixty-nine days and I came right here to Enyoh.

When we returned from leave I was sent to Enugu garrison camp and from there I was sent to the 68th Army General Hospital Yaba-Lagos and in September 1944 a message came from Burma that nurses were required at the battle field and I was sent there. We had passed through the Indian Ocean, Mediterranean Sea, Suez Canal and reached India. It took us five weeks to reach Bombay. From Bombay we had left by train to the old capital of India, Calcutta, and from there lorries came and took us towards the battle field. At the battle front everybody was asked to build or dig a trench. European soldiers dug theirs separately from ours. Then, from there, we trekked to some place and I was taught bomb traps and shown how enemies were setting them.

On 25 December 1944 it was then I saw wounded people when enemies opened fire on us. Three deaths had occurred. We were there for two weeks and the first Japanese war prisoners were brought and showed to us so that we would know their structure to be able to distinguish them from our soldiers. We were there fighting day and night inside the bush; and war equipment was supplied to us by a battalion of horses. This was taking place at the Arakan jungle and were there for ten and a half weeks. By the time we were suffering in the bush, they later told us that we would soon reach the motor road and that our suffering would soon finish; but at the road the enemies were in thousands and we had to employ anti-aircraft. I was the third person out of a thousand from the first two people that were shot but the sergeant Mr. Keke had shouted for me to get away from the soldiers who had been shot because as an army nurse I had gone to him to see if I could stop that soldier from excessive bleeding. At the road the Japanese were fierce and strong but our planes came bombing the Japanese and we were using anti-aircraft bombs protecting ourselves. We did this until we reached Tomadoh, and it was there that the battle was hand to hand and our people came with five tanks to help us since the enemies were refusing to retreat. It was there that one of our tanks was destroyed. It was there that we buried so many of our people about three in a grave. When we left from there and were going forward the enemies had written on a tree that "Six miles to Ann, you will not reach." This was when we had moved about four miles forward and it was there that things were hard and we had to withdraw. On returning I had used a hand grenade to kill an enemy.

Then eight planes came from India to relieve us because we had the center of attack. The planes had aimed at one corner and throwing bombs killing both the enemies and our own people and then we were able to have a chance to pass. Then we were taken to Tomadoh and there the Indian troops took ever. Because we had lost so many souls, the 82nd Division Memorial was built as a monument in memory of those who were killed at Tomadoh. One day at Tomadoh on 26 June 1945 at about two o'clock A.M. when I was on guard just in front of me I heard the noise of something like a generator steaming and I felt as if I was asleep and on turning on my right I saw a light showing some words which I couldn't read and there came a noise saying in Mungaka that if you keep my commandments your blessings shall be like man and sea. I don't know what made the noise. When we used to be at the battlefield every first of the month I wouldn't eat and would be praying for my life. At Gambia when people were buying medicine I would make a cross and wore it and on it I wrote "My savior is Jesus Christ."

I had been baptized when I was a small child and it was at the Lagos garrison that I received the First Holy Communion. While we were at Tomadoh we heard that the war had ended in Europe and that it was Emperor Hirohito of Japan that forced his army to surrender unconditionally. As we heard this we began to pray that God should bless him. But the Japanese had refused to stop fighting. Some of them had gone to the palace and committed suicide asking why they should surrender unconditionally.

Then we left to Rangoon, the capital of Burma. It was there that Captain Burden, a medical doctor, promoted me to Grade 2 nurse. Our major was called Woodroff. At Talwaldi our medical captain was Doctor Sair. We were at Talwaldi till some Japanese were brought as war prisoners. We were there for one year.

In December 1945 we left to Lagos. There we were taken to Ikeja Camp and there I was discharged from the army and my leave to end at 31 December 1946. While there the tradesmen were paid more than just the auxiliary army members. I was paid at overseas 115 pounds by the time I was leaving. At the battle we were never given any money.

They used to supply us with food from the air. They used to supply us biscuits and canned fish. From Ikeja I reached Victoria and then we came to Bamenda. Later I got married to that girl I had seen in Bafoucho but had lacked money to do so. By the time we were at Burma I had bought so many things which reached my home and were given to the girl's father as part of the dowry.

I had been awarded with medals: the Burma Star, Defense Medal, War Medal (1939–45) Star (and the Victoria Christ Medal). On discharge we were given resettlement books to reach and show the DO at Bamenda.

Later I was employed by the DO Bamenda as a Dispensary Attendant. That was in April 1948 and I worked at the Bamenda General Hospital and there I met Dr. Sair, who was with me in the army. The DO at Bamenda was Mr. Mill. I worked there for one year and was posted to Ndop.

From Ndop I was sent to open a dispensary at Nkambe. All along I was paid 7 pounds a month. From Nkambe I was sent to open another dispensary at Balikumbat, and in 1952 I wrote to resign because I was sick. From then I haven't gone out again and now work kola nuts and also manage life from the money which my children send to me.

I had three wives but two died. I had one from Balikumbat and one from Bafoucho and now this one from Enyoh here. The wife from Bafoucho had eight children, that from Enyoh had ten children but two died, and that from Balikumbat had one child.

Of all my children there is one who is a Professor at University of Yaoundé. He is teaching in the Department of Physics. There is another one Dr. Nkwende at the Bamenda General Hospital. There is one working at Bafoussam in the Preventative Department of Public Delegation Bafoussam, he is Michael Ajeck. There is also Sarah Tifu teaching at Government Nursing School Bamenda, There is also Peter Mba, who is a veterinary agent at Pinyin. The rest are still schooling. One has just completed high school and has passed GCE A/L in two papers. She is Mary Enjong; and two are in Government High School Mbengwi the first cycle.

An Interview in New York City

William D. Neufville, *St. Mary's, February 2007*
   William visited St. Mary's Church Hall on the Lower East Side of Manhattan many times in 2007. In conversation he mentioned that he had been in the British Army in Burma during World War II. Here are notes of one meeting. Later he moved to Staten Island and we never met again.

William was born in Liberia, at Cape Palmas, in 1927. His father sent him to school in Lagos first to Holy Cross Secondary School and then to St. Gregory's College. In his last year, 1941, he was "conscripted" for the British army. They stayed at a barracks, drilling. Later he took a troopship straight to Burma with the "Highland Brigade." He was an ammunition carrier for a tank division in the armored car brigade. Major General Orde Wingate was first, but he died in a glider accident (*he died when a US Mitchell bomber exploded*). Then Montbatten came in.

President King of Liberia treated the native people badly. Barclay was a mean person. There was no work in Liberia and so his father left his mother and went to Nigeria, where he worked with the PWD and the *Post and Telegraph* (P+T). Later he became a marine pilot. William started school in Liberia and then his father sent him to a Senior High School, St. Gregory, in Lagos. . . . In 1941, government employees were recruited first, then senior students in high school. At Kings College in Lagos the students protested by fasting on sugar and water. The young and strong were selected. He was tall and strong and so he was taken at St. Gregory College. At first he was in the 55th Brigade and later the regular army, 1st Battalion, Katsina Regiment. While in the army his benefits were sent to his family from a book. He had great respect for the Hausa in the regular army; they were uneducated but very brave.

Military chaplains were remembered by some of those interviewed, especially one Francis Woodman, a missionary from Manchester, who worked in the British Cameroons. In the next chapter we will learn something about Father Woodman and some others, Protestant and Catholic.

CHAPTER 8

Chaplains

I was at Mukuru when a message arrived: "Tom come for army."
—Thomas Go-oh Natang, Steward for Francis Woodman

And this explains why many of our own ex-servicemen always proudly referred to him as Major Woodman.
—Archbishop Verdzekov in his Memoriam of 27 September 1974

In an article titled *Faith in Wartime* an anonymous Mill Hill Missionary serving with African troops from East Africa in Burma reflected on his experience in the 11th East African Division:

It was during the Burma Campaign that the test was most severe. The enemy had been defeated at the epic battles of Imphal and Kohima, and the plan to conquer India was smashed; the monsoon was on in all its fury, rivers were swollen and roads impassable; it was necessary that the Japanese should be chased back to Central Burma. This force was 32 percent Catholic, and with it went missionaries of the White Fathers, Mill Hill, Holy Ghost, and Montfort Fathers. . . . A sight that was a constant source of astonishment to officers and men alike was that of the closely packed band of Catholics that would rapidly and quietly gather around the priest as he celebrated Holy Mass in the steaming dampness of the jungle. . . . To them a Rosary was an essential part of their equipment . . . home-made ones, deftly knotted from the cords of the parachutes that brought their rations . . . identification marks . . . to many a chaplain. . . . Example frequently succeeds where words fail. Thus, too, it was with the Askari. . . . The constancy of the Catholic to his prayers . . . and the many whose lives were exemplary to an incredible degree amidst the incessant temptations of military life—all this reaped a harvest of souls altogether beyond the hope of any missionary back in Africa. Upwards of 12,000 Askari (*name given to East African soldiers*) were received into the Church during those days, some whilst in training, and many more as they approached the danger zone of battle. . . . Mission stations are already opened, or are foremost in the plans of E. A. bishops, because of this unexpected increase of Catholics. Districts in which it would have been tedious and difficult to penetrate have already shown a demand for priests, due to the fervor of newly baptized ex-Askari. Such is an aftermath of war that is rarely contemplated by us at home. . . . As a grand reminder of the intensity of the light of faith that has shone throughout the darkness of war, the II (E.A.) Divisional Commander caused to be erected in the cathedral of the Jesuit Fathers at Ranchi, India, in which place the East Africans were training on VJ-Day: "To thank God for the favours He has bestowed upon the thousands of Africans from Kenya, Tanganyika, Nyassland, Uganda and Rhodesia who have worshipped in this church, and whom he has led to victory.[1]

Chaplains to the Royal West African Frontier Force[2]

At Gungong on the Bali-Batibo Road, Pius Mbasong, who was not a Catholic, remembered Fr. Woodman:

> We were there for one year and we were given a casual leave of seven days and we went to Jerusalem. . . . They used to go and show us all these places. Captain Francis Woodman was the Catholic chaplain. There were two chaplains. One for the Catholics and the other for the Presbyterians (Basel Mission). I cannot remember the name of the Presbyterian chaplain. You know it is almost forty years from then and I cannot more remember his name . . . (no matter) what kind of a church you will find it there (The Church of the Holy Sepulcher) and get the father and he would bless you. We were baptized by the father inside that church.[3]

Mill Hill Missionary Chaplains

Two Mill Hill Missionaries from the British Cameroons became military chaplains during World War II: Francis Woodman and John Ord. Father Blight, the senior military chaplain to the West African Frontier Force, met Fathers Ord and Woodman at Bamenda in 1943. Father Ord was sent to Gambia and Father Woodman was stationed first in Nigeria and then in North Africa.

John Ord

John Ord was born at Hartpool, England, 12 June 1909. He studied at Freshfield, 1925–1928, and Burn Hall near Durham, 1928–1930, in the UK, Roosendahl in the Netherlands, 1930–1932, and finally at St. Joseph's in Mill Hill, London, where he was ordained on 12 July 1936.

Appointed to Cameroon, he served missions at Tiko, Mankon, and Bafut. In February 1943 he joined the British army as a chaplain.

> I was commissioned into the Royal Army Chaplains Department to serve with the RWAFF with particular concern for Cameroon troops. After service in Nigeria, Sierra Leone, Gambia, and Gold Coast (now Ghana), I was appointed senior chaplain West Africa Command and stationed at GHQ Accra. This post I held from 1945 to 1950 when I was demobilized.

[*Letter to Superior General, MHM*
HQ West Africa Command]
America Camp
Accra
Gold Coast
West Africa]
... I will still have to serve in the Forces. Catholic troops in West Africa still need the services of chaplains and will for some time. There are no more being commissioned so we who are here must just stick on.
Gifford Camp, September 1948[4]

Francis Woodman

Francis Woodman was born in Manchester 17 December 1902. His father was John and his mother Jane Hanlon. He had four brothers and four sisters. He studied at the Mill Hill Missionary training centers at Freshfield in the UK, Roosendahl in the Netherlands, and Mill Hill in London. He was ordained 17 July 1927. His sister was a nun, Sister Jeane Therese, FMSJ.

He was at Mankon in Bamenda in 1943 when he was appointed chaplain to the RWAFF to serve in the Middle East.[5]

In his Memoriam of 27 September 1974 for Fr. Woodman, Paul Verdzekov, Archbishop of Bamenda wrote:

Father Francis Woodman
Permission: Mill Mill
Archive (MHA)

And this explains why many of our own ex-servicemen always proudly referred to him as Major Woodman.

Friday evening 27 September 1974, Fr. Francis Woodman quietly passed away at Njinikom. He was aged 72. ... With the death of Frankie as he was affectionately called by his fellow Millhillians, West Cameroon Catholics lose one of those veteran missionaries to whom the country owes so much ... who laid the foundation of the church in West Cameroon.

... he felt very much more at home in Njinikom than in his native Manchester.
... Francis Woodman served this country for 47 years. He now lies buried in Njinikom next to another well-beloved missionary, Fr. Thomas Burke Kennedy, who died there in 1951. They gave their lives for Cameroon. May they rest in peace.

According to his family tree his mother was the sister of Bishop Henry Hanlon, who left from England with four others for East Africa and Uganda in 1895. In 1943 he was appointed chaplain to "active service in the West African Frontier Force in the Middle East during the last war."

Fr. Francis Woodman, left in white shirt, with Frs. Sam Carney and
Matthew Nabben in Ikassa, 1930s. Permission: Mill Hill Archive
(MHA)

Francis Woodman returned to Cameroons in October 1946 and was
appointed to his former station at Baseng mission. Fr. Ord remained in the
army. In October 1948 he was the senior Roman Catholic chaplain to the British army in West Africa. There are many ex-servicemen in Cameroon who recall
Fr. Woodman from the time he was in North Africa or after when he encouraged the Ex-Servicemen's Association in Cameroon.

The name Fr. Francis Woodman was remembered in the stories told by old
soldiers in this book. For example, Peter Ntungwen of Bali-Nyonga knew Fr.
Woodman in Bamenda before the war and met him again in Libya where he was
chaplain. It was there Peter was baptized.

Chaplain Woodman organized a course of six months preparation for Baptism
for those soldiers who were interested. Simon Rela of Bafmeng was one of them,
and he was baptized by Father at Kasserine in 1943.

Thomas Go-oh tells his story elsewhere in this book. He served as Fr. Woodman's orderly in the army and continued to work for him for many years after the
war back in Cameroon.

Interview with an Auxiliary Chaplain

Leo van Son, 23 June 1987

One missionary served as what he called an auxiliary chaplain at Bota near
Victoria late in the War.

Father van Son was born 8 September 1911 in Waspik, the Netherlands. He
was ordained in London on 14 July 1935 by Cardinal Arthur Hinsley. He
taught at a minor seminary in Hooren in the Netherlands for two years before
being sent to the Cameroon mission. He joined a group of other missionaries in

Liverpool, where he boarded an Elder Dempster ship bound for West Africa. "I was given one pound, a helmet for the tropics, and a suit made by a brother that never fit. We were told to wear a suit and a Roman collar with all the colonial officers on board. I looked like no one on earth."

There were about 300 people. The ship was the HMS *Adda*. Fr. van Son was assigned to Bota Mission with "Old Jan Jansen." Bota had a "procure" for the mission and Leo was sent by launch over night to Calabar, arriving at three o'clock A.M. He would go sometimes with a push cart as far as Aba to buy stores like toilet paper, bulbs, and parts for parafin lamps. Bishop Moynagh was always good to missionaries who came, especially from Ikassa mission.

After 9 years in the British Cameroons, Fr. van Son said he was to go on home leave, back to Europe, probably in 1945, but there was no way to do so. There were no steamers from Victoria, and so he became an army chaplain at Bota. At the time there were 800 to 900 troops at Bota. "I was paid 40 to 50 pounds a month."

He went to see the director of the UAC, whom he knew, by army launch. He then got a train to Port Harcourt, where he met the captain of a Danish ship going to Rotterdam. There was no chance, but the captain did take him to Lagos, where he met the Dutch captain of the West Africa Line who took him along in record time. He spent fourteen months at home and had difficulty finding passage back to Cameroon. The return trip took forty-two days with a one-week stop in Antwerp and another week in Bordeaux. He arrived in Douala and took a launch to Tiko in British Cameroons.

Chaplains in the Middle East, North Africa, and Southern Europe, 1940–1943

For the Middle East Command the Senior Catholic Chaplain was Msgr. Joseph Stapleton. He had been an army chaplain since 1916. His jurisdiction covered Egypt, the Western Desert, Palestine, Syria, Cyprus, the Red Sea littoral, the Sudan, Eritrea, and for a time Iraq and Iran.

In 1940 there were fewer than thirty chaplains. By 1943 there were 154. An Infantry Brigade chaplain was responsible for the Catholics in the brigade. They also ministered to prisoners of war. There were over 100,000 Italian prisoners of war in the Middle East. This is where Francis Woodman served.[6]

Chaplains in Burma and the Far East

In February 1944, the 14th Army went on the offensive, first in Arakan, then in March and April at Imphal and Kohina.

Father James O'Carroll of Kilmore was Senior Chaplain to the Forces (SCF), Roman Catholic (RC), India Command, and Fr. J. A. Gardner, of Westminster, became SCF (RC) South East Asia Command.

At the Battle of Kohima, Fr. James G. Callaghan from Hexam/Newcastle Diocese, attached to Worcester's 5th Brigade, 2nd Division, was killed and buried at Kohima War Cemetery.

Ten months from the beginning of the offensive, hard fighting brought the British, India, and Africa troops to the banks of the Irrawaddy:

> . . . long marches thick jungle. . . . I rode mules. I swam rivers. The most terrible thing was the rattling of the bullets and their ricocheting off the trees. You would often get lost—even if you were very close to your comrades. You would have four or five hundred men clearing a path in front of you with hatchets cutting down the undergrowth so we could follow with the mules.

With the exception of the Allied armies in Italy, the 14th Army was probably the most polyglot of all armies in the Second World War . . . among the King's African Rifles . . . East Africa, Kenya, Uganda, Tanzania . . . of the 11th Division. . . . Among the Catholic chaplains was Fr. Tom Maher CSSp.[7]

George Appleton, the archdeacon of the Anglican Church in Burma wrote about the liberation of Burma and encounters with military chaplains:

> The first S.P.G. [Society for the Propagation of the Gospel] station was liberated in January 1944, when British troops entered Shwebo. Two Burmese priests, Po Loo and Chit Htway, had carried on quietly and faithfully, in spite of great difficulties. The splendid mission buildings erected by the veteran missionary Stockings, were almost undamaged and were taken over immediately as headquarters of the Civil Affairs Service (military government). The church had been stripped of all its furniture and fittings, but the military chaplain, with a body of soldiers, soon had it clean and ready for worship again.
>
> An interesting story is told of a Roman Catholic village near Shwebo, in which the Christians discovered that there was an R.C. chaplain with the troops. They approached him and asked for a Mass of Thanksgiving. By some accident he had got separated from his Communion vessels, but the Christians were not at all disturbed by this news. They went away and returned a short while later, bringing with them the vessels of their own small church, which they had buried at the approach of the Japanese, nearly three years before. The next morning the whole village came to Mass with grateful thanks for their liberation. We are not told what the Gradual was, but it may well have been Psalm 126:
>
> > When the Lord turned again the captivity of Sion:
> > then were we like unto them that dream.
> > Then was our mouth filled with laughter:
> > and our tongue with joy.

In March 1945, Mandalay and Maymyo were freed; these were both strong Anglican centres. At Mandalay a little group of Burmese Christians had remained near the Winchester Mission; their first question was, "How is Saya-gyi Garrad? Where is he now?" Most of the buildings escaped destruction. Christ Church was stripped inside, like almost all other churches, but strangely enough the font was left. This had been presented by Queen Victoria to the original wooden church built by King Mindon for Dr. Marks. The main building of the Children's Hospital is also undamaged.[8]

The retreat and defeat of the Japanese in Burma was celebrated in the capital, Rangoon, in August 1945. Included in the rejoicing was a grand thanksgiving service that took place in the Anglican cathedral of the Holy Trinity. We have a description of the event by a Church of England missionary in the next chapter.

CHAPTER 9

Thanksgiving in Rangoon and Return to West Africa, 1945, 1946

The Bishop returned to Rangoon in July, and his first great function was a service of cleansing for the Cathedral, which had been used by the Japanese as a factory for sauce and "saki" (toddy). The Cathedral was crowded with members of the three Services and Burma Christians, and the Bishop, with his attendants, went in procession round the Cathedral sprinkling blessed water on building and people alike.
 —George Appleton, Society for the Propagation of the Gospel, London

Now that the operations in which you have been engaged in Burma have been so successfully completed and your return to your home country is imminent, I wish to acquaint all officers, N.C.O.s and men of the 81st West African Division of my sincere appreciation and gratitude for their outstanding services in fighting for the liberation of Burma.
 —Louis Mountbatten, Supreme Allied Commander,
  South East Asia Command, 26 July 1945.[1]

With the liberation of Burma and World War II nearing an end, it was a time of restoration in Rangoon. The 82nd Division was still in the country, while the 81st Division had already been withdrawn to India. The troops of the 82nd Division were to participate in the thanksgiving and remembrance services in Rangoon during July and August.

The Holy Trinity Anglican Cathedral was restored in 1945. The Bishop had returned in July, cleansed the cathedral, and held a great thanksgiving service for the victory over the Japanese a few days later. Electricity failed and so the army lined up twenty jeeps outside and shined their lights through the windows. One jeep was even driven into the Cathedral so that everyone could read the service papers.

West African troops, most likely from the 82nd Division, at the thanksgiving service, St. Mary's Cathedral, Rangoon, Burma, August 1945. Source: Imperial War Museum

RECONCILIATION SERVICE

The Anglican Bishop of Rangoon, Dr. George West, led the service and preached the sermon. There were prayers to cleanse and restore the Cathedral for use. A member of the Karen tribe read the lesson in English and Burmese.

Prayer and psalms rang out through the shattered stained-glass windows of the little red brick Gothic cathedral of Rangoon on Saturday, when nearly 1,000 men and women of the Services, as well as Burmese civilians, attended a unique Anglican re-dedication service. The service was simple, solemn, and sincere, in this sacred place which the Japanese had used as a brewery, a byre for cattle, and a stable for mules. The invaders had sunk great vats in the stone floor, and had fermented their wine in the nave. Organ, pulpit, altar, and pews had been torn out by Air Force personnel, and the Royal Engineers had patched and mended to restore the Cathedral as a fitting place once more for public worship.[2]

Men of the Royal West African Frontier Force who lost their lives in these campaigns are buried in cemeteries in Kenya, Abyssinia, and Burma. Those whose graves were not found, or if found are so situated that permanent maintenance is not possible, are commemorated by name on the memorials at Nairobi and Rangoon. West Africans who died while serving in the Middle East lie in cemeteries in Egypt and Libya, or are individually commemorated on the Alamein Memorial; and there are more than 450 West African war graves in various cemeteries in India where these troops were trained, rested, and re-formed. Men who died while serving with the Forces in West Africa whose graves are not known, or are unmaintainable, are commemorated by name on memorials in the countries of their enlistment; the Nigerians at Lagos, men of the Gold Coast (Ghana) at Accra, of Gambia at Bathurst and of Sierra Leone at Freetown.

Lord Louis Mountbatten held a victory parade in Rangoon on 15 June 1945. Cathedral in the background. Thanks to Yangontimemachine.com.

Holy Trinity Anglican Cathedral, Rangoon. Source: WikiCommons

Barnaby Phillips describes the return to Africa of a hospital ship carrying wounded West Africans:

In the middle of March, Isaac and David were on the dockside at Bombay, surrounded by other wounded West Africans, all waiting to board a hospital ship for home. Some of the men were blind. Some had lost limbs. Others seemed to be mentally incapacitated. More than a year and a half had passed since the West African contingents had disembarked on those same docks with the task of protecting the British Empire from the Japanese invaders. Each of these men had survived the Burma campaign, but some had been broken in the process.[3]

The return journey for the West Africans from Burma took the men through the Suez canal and Mediterrranean and down the West Coast of Africa.

Peter Ntungwen of Balinyonga described his final days in India, where the 81st Division had been withdrawn from the fighting in Burma:

Then we were preparing to go to Japan after that war in Burma had finished. We prepared for two weeks and then Japan surrendered with the two atomic bombs that were dropped by America. So we couldn't go to Japan again since they surrendered. So we stayed for some months and were sent to West Africa. We never again passed through South Africa but through Gibraltar before arriving in West Africa. It took us 15 days to reach Lagos. At Lagos we went to the demobilization camp at Ekeja and we were given rest of seven days. And we went to Lagos town to spend these days there.

From Lagos the soldiers returned to Victoria in the British Cameroons. From there Peter with others carried on to Bamenda.

CHAPTER 10

Remembrance Day in Bota Gardens, 1999

Cameroon Service of Remembrance and Dedication, Limbe, November 1999
Address of welcome: The British High Commissioner
Laying of Wreath by the British High Commissioner, Last Post (bugle call) Two
minutes silence
Reveille (bugle call)
Laying of wreath by representative of the fraternal union of Cameroon
ex-servicemen of the crown
Laying of poppies by ex-servicemen
                                        —Official Program, 1999

The grand thanksgiving service celebrated in Rangoon in July of 1945 was repeated in a simple dignified ceremony in the Bota Botanical Gardens of Cameroon on 11 November 1999. There are at least twenty graves of veterans maintained in the Botanical Garden Cemetery in Limbe. British ex-servicemen in the remnants of their World War II uniforms, with campaign medals prominent, mixed with veterans of the Cameroon Armed Forces. The Anglican Bishop of Douala led a prayer, wreaths were laid, and tributes given.

Afterwards there was a reception at the Ex-Servicemen's Club in Limbe. It was there that I sat with some of the ex-servicemen to record briefly details of their service. As the reception continued, the volume increased until it was no longer possible to hear well. Some of the men also thought I was there to interview them concerning pension awards that they said they were promised but never received. But despite disappointment they were very kind and shared their documents and stories, and allowed a photograph to be taken.

Mr. Scott of the Cameroon Development Corporation, an organizer of the service, welcomed us that day in 1999.[1]

The British Legion, an organization that gives advice and support to veterans, sponsors the Remembrance Day, which is held each year at the Commonwealth War Graves in the Gardens.

In 1892, when Cameroon was a German colony called Kamerun, the gardens were set aside. Originally it was an experimental place where useful tropical species were tested—rubber, coffee, cocoa, oil palm, banana, teak, and sugar cane among them. At one time it was considered one of the most important botanical gardens in the world. Under British mandate from 1920 to 1932 it was connected to Kew Gardens in England. Until 1958 it was staffed by Cameroonians. Since 1988 it has worked in partnership with the UK and now has 120 acres of land.

In the garden site there is a small military cemetery with several graves from the Commonwealth: four from World War I and sixteen from World War II.

Commonwealth War Graves Cemetery, Botanical Gardens, Limbe, Cameroon.
Photo: R. O'Neil

The service began at 10:45 A.M. with prayers by the Anglican bishop of Douala in Cameroon.

Interviews, Bota, 11 November 1999 at the Ex-Serviceman's Club, Limbe, from 11:30 A.M.

One of those present was Sebastian Fonjoh, the President of the Fraternal Order of Cameroon Ex-Servicemen of the Crown; he led the delegation from Bamenda. He joined the Nigerian army on 20 July 1952. He spoke of his senior brother Tacho, who was in the Burma campaign. His brother returned in 1946 and was "reengaged" in the Nigerian army, taking Sebastian to Kaduna. He served until 1966 and the Biafran War. He was with Colonel Ojuku at Enugu.

Ex-Servicemen's Club, Limbe, 2024.
Thanks to B. Forkwa

Ex-Servicemen's Guest House, Bamenda, ca. 2000.
Photo: R. O'Neil

Photos on pp. 105–111: R. O'Neil

Andrew Neng

Andrew Neng was born at Wum in about 1926. His father was Gabriel Anong and his mother Frances Isih. He was a schoolboy at Njinikom with Fr. Jacobs, who baptized him. He never completed Standard 6, leaving in Standard 5.

"I was working for the Mabeta plantation when I joined the army at Victoria in 1943. We trained in Zaria for six months before leaving for Lagos and then to Freetown and after two months reached Egypt." He trained as a military policeman. He served for three years in the army: in Burma and India, Benghazi, Ismalia, and Alexandria. When the war finished he returned to Cameroon around July 1946. At home he worked for the PWD for four years and then went back to the Nigerian army for six years. He had a Burma Star, a Defense Medal, a Victory Medal and an East Africa Star. He was also President of the Ex-Servicemen of Wum, where there were 200 members.

Simon Achu Fundoh

Simon Achu Fundoh was born in November 1914 at Kasu Qt, Wum. His father was Fundah and his mother Njangasa. He was baptized in the Presbyterian Church (*Basel Mission*) at the coast in 1940. He worked at the Esongo CDC (Cameroon Development Corporation) plantation.

In 1942 he joined the army at was sent directly to The Gambia. After going on leave he went to India. He was in Burma. He only remembered "Major Bull." He was in the army for "3 years, 53 days." After returning to Cameroon in 1945 he stayed at home for two years before going back to the coast and the CDC. He later went back to Wum, where he married two women and had nine children. His Discharge Card noted the Burma Star, the Africa Star, and the Service Star. "Loyal Service," signed by R. L. Bond.

Joseph Musanga

Joseph Musanga was born at Nkoramujang near Wum in the North West Region of Cameroon. His father was Aboh and his mother was Efosi. He finished Standard 2 in Wum. He was baptized at Bota in 1952 by Fr. Sullivan. He was working at the Mbeme plantation. He entered the army on 9 September 1942. They trained outside Limbe (Victoria). He went to Akapa, Lagos, and then to the Middle East. He was in Tripoli and Benghazi. He remembered Captain Pickett. When the war was over they had seven days' leave in Jerusalem and then back to Benghazi before going home.

At home he was a CDC overseer for seven years. He married Anna and had seven children. His card: L. D. Joseph Mesanga, #LN/16410, 2411 Battalion, Corporal, buglar.

Simon Wanji

Simon Wanji was born at Bangante. He was baptized a Presbyterian in 1939 and worked on a plantation in Loum. From Loum, he joined the army, first training near Victoria in 1942. They sailed to Calabar and then to Lagos before going on to Egypt and the Suez Canal.

He worked for Customs in Limbe from 1946, before becoming a trader, buying and selling clothes. He had three medals.

Francis Njilifack

Francis Njilifack was from Manyu Division. He joined the army in 1943 (#93682) and went to Nigeria-Aba and Lagos and then to Egypt, where he was a driver. Later he went to Baghdad. They guarded prisoners.

He returned to Cameroon in 1946 and was a driver for the CDC for nineteen years, and then the Highways for two years.

He was baptized in Tiko in 1937. He married Agnes and had seven children. He was awarded two war medals.

1999: c/o Cassava Farm, Limbe

Pius Ntouko

Pius Ntouko was born in 1925 at Banti, Bafang. His father was Yonga and his mother was Ndze. He had no schooling. He was not working when he joined the army. He went to South Africa, Italy, and Burma. He was in #2720 Regiment, 2nd Division. He had four medals including the Africa Star and the Burma Star.

When he returned he worked for the CDC as a "watchnight." He was baptized in Burma in 1946 as a Catholic. He married Paulina and had four children.

George Ndumbe

George Ndumbe was born at Buea in 1917. He joined the army in 1942 and was baptized a Catholic by Fr. Woodman at Benghazi.

Dominic Tazoh

From the Royal West African Frontier Force Discharge Book:

D/4520, 5 years, enlisted at Bota 1/4/41

Regiment NA 38324

Sawyer

Discharged 31 March 1946, age 27. Awards: 1939–45 Star, Burma Star, Defense Medal, Med. 1939–1945

Payments at discharge: 44 pounds 11 shillings 11 pence.

George Nkum Dinga

George Nkum Dinga was born at Esu in 1921. His father was Dinga. He went to Government School, Bamenda, and then completed Standard 6 at Soppo. He joined the army in 1941 at Limbe. He went first to Enugu and Ghana for training. He was trained for the Signal Corps at Achimota College. He first went to the Middle East and then to India and Burma. In 1944 he was in Freetown, Sierra Leone.

When he returned he was employed by the Post Office, Bamenda. He was baptized by Fr. Matthew Nabben, a Mill Hill Missionary, in Bamenda in1951. He married Rufina and had ten children. He retired from the Post Office in 1979.

His Discharge Book: NA 209218

Burma Star, Defense Medal, Africa Star
Corporal; discharged:1 March 1947; 3 years, 233 days.

Kum Marcus Etche

Kum Marcus Etche was born at Esu, in Menchum Division of the North West Region. His
father was Chi. He served in Egypt, Alexandia,
and Tripoli. He went on leave to see Jerusalem
and Bethlehem.

He was a "waterman" at Cassava Farm. He had
the Burma Star, the Defense Medal, and two
other medals.

Joseph Abang

Joseph Abang was born at Babanki Tungo in
1918. In 1936 he went to Nigeria and joined the
army at Calabar on 15 March 1942. He had
worked for a "white man" in Calabar and traveled through Nigeria and Cameroon. He served
in Egypt for two years as a "mess servant." Once
he went on leave to "Israel."

When he returned Nigeria in 1946 he worked
for the Eastern Nigeria Corporation. He was in
charge of an oil mill for fourteen years. He spent
twenty-six years in Nigeria before returning to
Cameroon in 1963, where he worked for the
CDC for ten years.

He married his first wife Mary and had three
children. He married a second wife, Odelia.

Joseph Njuma (now Joseph Ewoke)

Joseph Njuma (Ewoke) was born in 1924 at Buea. His father was Nathaniel Njuma and his mother was Namundu. He went to the Basel Mission School but never finished Standard 6.

In 1942 he joined the army at Limbe. He went to Enugu for training and then on to Lagos before sailing to Egypt. He was baptized in Egypt in the Church of England. He spent 4 years and 9 months in the army before returning to Cameroon in 1946. He was a "gunner." He had "ribbons".

He worked with the CDC from 1951 to 1985. He married Frida and had eight children.

Lucas Ngalle Nganje

Lucas Ngalle Nganje was born in 1923. He was from Bakwere, Ekona. He is a Baptist. According to his Discharge Book he was a Lance Corporal, gunner. 3441 Coy RWAFF.

He went to Lagos for six months and then to The Gambia and Dakar before sailing to Egypt, Tripoli, and Alexandria. He was discharged in 1946 at Lagos.

At home he had no job except for being a "watch night" (*watchman*) and doing small jobs. He married and had two children.

Joseph Ngembu (ill)

One veteran was sick and unable to be present, but he sent his book. He was Joseph Chu Ngembu, from Momo Division of the North West Region.

Discharge Book: He enlisted 24 December 1942. Reg #AIA 38059.

Final assessments: Military conduct, very good.

Testimonial of Corporal Joseph Chu: "Efficient at his work. Good nature and cheerful. Smart and clean in his appearance. Is of trustworthy, reliable and sober disposition. He is loyal to his superiors.

Special Force: "You came out from the middle of Burma where you have done your job in a manner which has thrilled the whole world."

26 March 1944 (signed) Major General Mastinque(?), Cmd. Special Force (*known as the "Chindits"*), Ngembu earned the 1939–45 Star, Burma Star, Defense Medal, War Medal 1939–45

He served 5 years, 159 days; 2 years, 204 days overseas

Trade foreman

Discharge: 31 May 1945, 12 Battalion Nigeria Regiment
Amount paid 37.14.5

Daniel Ndeke

According to notes, Ndeke's brother was
in Burma.

Unidentified Veterans Interviewed

Stone placed in front of tree in Bota Gardens:
John Maxwell Edmonds, 1875–1958
"When you go home tell them of us and say,
for your tomorrows these gave their today"

This tree was planted on 12 November 1995 by the British High Commissioner Mr. Nicholas McCarthy, OBE, to commemorate the fiftieth anniversary of the end of the Second World War.

Epilogue

Seldom did any veteran mention the violence and death they witnessed, or the loss of comrades, especially in Burma.

Killingray quotes a former soldier of the Gold Coast Regiment in Burma: "This jungle war was not child's play—it was something very dangerous." Joseph Ndikum said simply, "Sometimes we walked on blood," and added that the war, especially in Burma, was the "No Small Thing" of the title. Taken from the Pidgin, the expression fit for most veterans. Their time in the army was something important but not easily described, yet it was very serious. That was it. Looking at their documents and listening to them recall their time during World War II, one is first impressed by the years that were taken from a young man's life. It could be four years or more. It was not a dream but real life represented in the medals and discharge cards.

There are photographs very often used to show Africans serving in the British Army during the war. They are usually of cheerful, smiling young men at ease or marching, carrying their equipment in North Africa or Burma.

To show a more serious side, one photograph used in this book was taken in August 1945 of the men of the 82nd division pictured with the returned Anglican bishop of Rangoon. Quiet, neat, hats in hand, they joined in the cathedral to give thanks with other troops that they had survived the war and to remember their comrades who did not. The other photo, used on the cover, is a veteran, who, even after fifty years, is in a neat uniform, calm and dignified. See the expression in his eyes. He is a man and worthy of respect.

Professor Ndi considers the story of these men as a way to introduce questions "begging for explanation and justification" about what they were "fighting for and losing their lives for."

As this is being written the *New York Times* had long articles about two places in Africa where questions are being asked about the past. One, on December 2, was about the eightieth anniversary of the killing of unarmed West African soldiers who fought for France and were prisoners of war for years. They were on their way home, staying in a camp outside of Dakar, Senegal, waiting for promised compensation. The place is called Camp Thiaroye. Children at the school built on the site asked: "Why were they massacred? How were they killed?" They wanted to know more.

President Biden was visiting Angola, an area that for hundreds of years was the source of enslaved people taken to the Americas. It is estimated that one quarter of all the enslaved Africans in the United States came from this area. Speaking of slavery, the president said: It should be faced. It is our duty to face our history—the good, the bad, and the ugly, the whole truth. That's what great nations do."

Angolan historians are trying to raise awareness among their own people about this history. One said that whenever he gave lectures about the atrocities endured by the enslaved as they were sold to the ships, Angolans "became visibly angry." The article concludes that the time is correct for asking questions.

We have the stories told by a small number of men from the former British Cameroons. Their names have been recalled and their stories told.

We close with the names of some who never returned. They are selected from the records of the Commonwealth War Graves Commission.

Belo Bamenda, private, 3rd Battalion, died 30 January 1945, Burma, buried in Rangoon.

Ajoh Bamesinge, 4th Battalion, d. 9 October 1944, Chittagong War Cemetery, Bangladesh

Bu Bamenda, private, 6th Battalion, d. 11 March 1941, Nigeria

Che Bamenda, 4th Battalion, d. 22 July 1941, Nigeria

Fineboy Babisi, 12th Battalion, d. 14 April 1944, Burma

Fineglas Bali, private, d. 20 December 1943, Yola

Gabriel Oshia, private, 7th WF Aux Group, d. 24 November 1945, Burma

Gata Bamessing, private, 4th Battalion, d. 16 October 1941, Nigeria

Hans Ngwa, 6th Battalion, d. 17 April 1942, Nigeria

Jamquam Bikom, 4th Battalion, d. 15 January 1945, Burma

Johnson Mamfe, d. 25 March 1945, Madras, India

Joseph Tanya, 4th Battalion, d. 16 January 1944, Burma

Marcus Lapido, 4th Battalion, d. 21 February 1944, Kirkel, India

Martin Itapa, 4th Battalion, d. 3 April 1944, Burma

Martin Fungom, 4th Battalion, d. 22 February 1944, Bangladesh

Mbang Banyo, 6th Battalion, d. 1 May 1942, Nigeria

Mekom Bamisinge, 4th Battalion, d. 22 January 1944, Burma

Munfu Bambalang, 6th Battalion, d. 7 November 1945, Madras, India

Nya Bamenda, 6th Battalion, d. 4 November 1943, Pune, India

Philip Mansi, 4th Battalion, d. 29 February 1944, Burma

Sam Bamenda, 4th Battalion, d. 13 October 1942, Nigeria

Samuel Neba Fobewe, 2nd Battalion, WA Aux Group d. 7 May 1945, Burma

Tabby Awoh, 4th Battalion, d. 30 January 1944, Burma

Tiko Bamenda, 9th Battalion, d. 31 October 1943, Nigeria

Wanea Bagango, private, 4th Battalion, d. 10 January 1944, Burma.

Yonas Nge, private, d. 2 March 1944, Burma

Hartsdale, NY
December 5, 2024

From an Officer Who Served in Burma with the 81st Division

Mr. Thomas A. Bruin was a friend of Fr. John Ball, a Mill Hill Missionary who was on the staff at St. Joseph's College, Mill Hill, London.

Thomas A. Bruin: additional notes
18 Woodcroft
Winchmore Hill
London N 21 3QP
0181 886 3184
May 20, 2008

Thomas Bruin was born in Glasgow in April 1915. His father, John, came from Dublin as an infant and his mother was Mary Roberts from North Wales.
He grew up in St. Peter's parish and went to St. Aloysius College, leaving at age 15. The following is based on an interview in his home in North London in May of 2008.

My father had a tailoring and clothing business. I joined him in 1930 during the depression. I learned a lot and studied accountancy at evening classes in Glasgow. I heard of a new organization, a government scheme operated by the coal owners and it had a secretariat. It was called the Scottish Coal Mine Scheme of 1936. Roman Catholics at that time had limited opportunities. With the help of a Protestant lecturer, I got a job from mid-1936 until 6 April 1940. It was a Saturday and I heard Lord Lovatt and Lovatt's Scouts (*a Scottish Highland Regiment*). He was in town and looking for recruits, mostly country people. I had an interview and he gave me a note for the recruiting office. When I got there I was told I would have to leave that night. I phoned my boss as I had the keys to the safe. "The army was very rigid. I have to leave tonight."

It was a three-days' journey to Newark in Notts. I found an open car on a goods train to Newark "it smelled of fish."

First there was basic training and then I was sent to regimental staff; there were thirty of us. At HQ I did typing and answered telephones.

I spent one year in the Farroes as an acting lance corporal (that is unpaid at that rank). It was Sudero Island , the lower tip where no troops had been before. There were ten to twelve of us. The school master greeted us. He took us into his home. He had a great collection of books and he told me about the earliest days of the Irish monks.

I was posted to another place, boarding a mail boat to return as a possible officer, but at Ft. George my papers were lost and I stayed there until 1941. I saw a notice that there was a need for officers in the Indian army. I was interviewed in Edinburgh: "What sport did you play," they asked. And I grew up in the tenements. "Cricket? Hockey?" My papers sent me to Aldershot. Then I had seven days embarkation leave. After Aldershot assembly, I returned to Glasgow to embark for India, by convoy. We assembled in the Clyde estuary. There were two aircraft carriers and frigates. Captain Digby Best, later admiral, was there. Zigzagging we went to West Africa stopping at Freetown, Sierra Leone, and then on to South Africa. The convoy split between Cape Town and Durban. We spent several days in Durban. I was invited to the home of a Dutch family. The next stage was to Bombay in 1942. Japan had a battle fleet in the area.

From Bombay we went to Bangalore. It was hot and arid. The Agram Plain was nicknamed Agony Plain.

Our general was General Festen, an RC, who got on well with General Joseph Stillwell of the United States.

We spent four months in Bombay and then suddenly we were treated as officers. To pass out we took an Urdu exam; I started preparing on the ship going out.

I had a choice of three regiments and chose Baluchistan, Patans, Punjabis and Donga Brahims. In October 1943 we were on the railway from Calcutta; it was used to supply China. We reached Imphal near the border. The Burma army was the forgotten army. We heard that the regiment was in the Chin Hills, 200 plus miles from the end of the railway. From there it was a single track road.

At Tiddim we had our first introduction when we met the wounded coming down the road.

In December/January 1941 we were back to milestone 41. Imperial Black Cat 17th Indian Division was chased from Burma in 1942 and lost half of the Division. I was in a mounted recon battalion.

Then I was sent back to camp for two months to train forces in mountain tactics.

My brother turned up. He was posted to the Indian army and sent up with an advanced company to Imphal. A call came on the field telephone, "Its your brother." We had 48 hours together. We went to a small Baptist mission.

Christmas 1943: the Brahmins and Muslims asked about celebrations at Christmas. When I arrived lonely on Christmas Eve and came back to mile 41 in the dark before daybreak to bamboo and elephant grass huts I saw small lights go up in front of the huts and there was food waiting for us.

In January/February 1944 I rejoined the battalion in the Chin Hills. One company had been attacked in force. It was not reckoned on. There were officers leading a Banzai charge. Our field guns turned them back. Mostly we were on patrol and we began seeing heavy columns of Japs going north.

I had seen West Africans at Ranchi in India. They were big strong fellows. Invited to a military tattoo they made smart troops. They did exercises on motorcycles, like on horseback, several men on one machine. I also saw some later in Rangoon near the end of the war.

In 1945 an edict came out that no one within six months of discharge was to be promoted. I was not paid but was a major and company commander. I was only paid as a captain on official discharge.

Tom Bruin: additional notes

There were two West African Divisions. Both fought in West Burma in the Arakan area.

The 81st Division arrived early in 1942. It was the first division involved. They built a route down the Kaladan Valley and engaged Japanese troops, supplied by "free dropping."

They rested during the summer of 1944 and reentered the same area in August 1944. Much of the route had to be rebuilt after the monsoon. We linked up with the 82nd Division in battles with the retreating enemy until the spring of 1945.

One African soldier remarked: "Bullet no fear, mortar no fear. But one bag rice come chop me. My wife thinks I be very foolish man."

World War II and British Cameroons from the Buea Archives

The news that Primus Forgwe is no longer with us is a sad blow to us all. He was a truly good man who for years unstintingly devoted his time and notable skills to the Cameroon National Archives, at times at cost of his health. I am sure you will agree that scholars, at home and abroad, as well as the Cameroon community at large, are greatly indebted to him, as will those yet to come.
— Correspondence: Shirley Ardener, 23 August 2020

Documents from the National Archive at Buea complement the testimony of contributors to this story. A first contact with the Buea Archive was in 1984. Interest was especially in District Officer assessment reports of the 1920s and 1930s of the Bamenda Grassfields. The late Father John Kubuo helped to retrieve, copy, and mail documents during the 1980s. In 2009 I visited and searched files at the archive concerning German Kamerun and the World War II years in British Cameroons. Research assistant of many years, Ben Forkwa, continued the search, copying relevant material. In 2014 Mr. Primus Forgwe was back at work in the "annex" and we met again. He returned to the NW Region and his home in Meta, where he died in 2020.

Primus Forgwe spoke about the founding of the archive on various occasions. For example once in a *YouTube* video, and another time to a journalist.

He had a great affection for Dr. Edwin Ardener and his wife, whom he spoke of as "Mama" Shirley. Dr. Ardener died in 1987. Forgwe referred to Dr. Ardener as the champion of the archive. It was thanks to the Ardeners and the Cameroon Government that the archive exists. The Ardeners had come to the former West Cameroon in 1953 to write about the plantations and the history of the local Bakweri people. When they arrived they found that the documents from colonial times were not in good condition. They had all been dumped in the old secretariat building. With the permission of the government, they determined to rescue the files that they found.

The first Cameroonian who worked with them was the late Pa Joseph Kima. They gathered together all the documents and brought them to the present Buea military headquarters. At that time it was a Native Authoriy primary school. The archives started in 1960. Between 1967 and 1969 the present building was constructed and in mid-1969 the then Prime Minister of West Cameroon, Hon. Solomon Tandeng Muna, officially opened the new archive. At first the archive was under the Secretariat of State for Primary Education. Now it is under the Ministry of Culture. Interesting to note that the ordinance went back to 1970 and Dr. Zachariah M. Njeuma . . . was the first Director of the West Cameroon Archives. After him was Mr. Bernard Ayuk, an anthropologist.[1]

Research in the archive was a success. Letters and reports were found by research assistant, Ben Forkwa. They often connected the interviews with the colonial administration of the British Cameroons during the war, often in very personal ways.

Primus Forgwe holding a photograph of Shirley Ardener.
Photo: R. O'Neil

Primus Forgwe at his desk in the Archive.
Photo: R. O'Neil

Selections from the Buea Archive, 1939–1947

In an annual report for the League of Nations under the title Defense of Territory:

> On the 25th of April 1939 a force of the Nigerian Police under the command of two European officers was sent to Victoria where it remained to assist in the defense of the territory until 27th August 1939 when its place was taken by one company of the 3rd Battalion, Nigerian Regiment Royal West African Frontier Force numbering five Europeans and 165 Africans. The 3rd Battalion handed over to the 5th Battalion in November 1939.
>
> At the same time, before the War broke out fifty-two younger elements on the German plantations fled to Fernando Po taking with them two motor barges, the property of the plantation. The remaining German nationals retained their former duties as employees of the British Supervisor of the plantations.

The report also mentions that the HMS *Rochester* visited Victoria from 29 April until the 1st of May.

In the annual report for 1940, WEH Hunt comments on the continued loyalty of the Province. All the "Divisions have their branches of the Defense

Force" and Bamenda was "particularly efficient." In addition the "sum of 1,875 pounds has been contributed to the "win the war" fund.

One document describes the Mamfe Unit of the "Nigeria Defense Force." Two Europeans are listed: W. D. Spence, the District Officer, and S. B. Sheldrick, Manager of the United Africa Company, Mamfe. The rest, twenty-five, are Africans. Among them is T. Kima from Bakabe, Mamfe, an interpreter. His special qualification was that he "can use rifle" and "has shot a gun." R. E. Effange from Buea was a 2nd class clerk who had shot a gun and was formerly of the Post and Telegraphs and "can operate telegraph." Achi Wum was a warder from Wum and an ex-soldier who could "handle a Lewis gun." S. Orok from Ossing was a bricklayer, and Abia of Amassi a P. A. Messenger. M. Ambe from Bali had been a headman and station laborer. There was also J. Doba from Balikumbat. The list ends with O. Kubiangha of Calabar, a teacher with the Education Department who "has shot a gun" but not yet proven because he was on leave.

Correspondence from the Commanding Officer of the Nigeria Regiment, Enugu, to the District Officer, Tiko, is dated 22 November 1939. He lists the names of reservists who had not reported to Enugu Reservists Training Centre. He writes, "Will you please cause enquiries to be made and these men apprehended if found and inform this office." All thirteen are connected with Nigeria but two are linked to the Cameroons. Corporal Lefo Balikumbat was probably from Bamenda but had an address in Calabar. Another had a Nigerian name, Momadu Yola, but with an address in Tiko.

A letter to the Resident from the police office in Buea dated 22 August 1940 informs the Resident that Mr. Bell was moving through the Province enlisting "carriers" for the army.

On 13 October 1941, Mr. C. J. Pence informed the Divisional Office that Joseph Nana No. 38089 of the 12th Battalion had been discharged from the army and issued "the necessary travelling warrants" at Port Harcourt to take him from Aba to Oron and then to Calabar and Victoria.

Another document had a hand-drawn map of the coast of British Cameroons marking places where troops could be landed (see next page).

The Mamfe Division Annual Report for 1942: Recruitment and Discipline

The DO reported that in August 1942 Lt. Watt and in November Lt. Blay visited the area to search for recruits for the Pioneer Corps.

Hand-drawn map of the coast of British Cameroons.
Source: Buea Archive

Two soldiers from the division had been visiting villages trying to enlist recruits. Their orders were to send 500 recruits from Mamfe, but during the year they sent the following: 11 from Bamenda Division, 49 from Mamfe Divison, 12 from the French Cameroons, and 95 Nigerians for a total of 167 recruits.

The DO also reported that soldiers passing through Mamfe on leave gave a lot of trouble in the area seizing foodstuffs and livestock either without paying or paying just a small amount.

One soldier, a native of Mbembe in Bamenda, was beaten seriously for stealing fish caught by a leper and arrived in Mamfe with two black eyes.

In another incident four Boki soldiers beat a village head, seized two sheep and terrorized a number of people. The four soldiers were arrested on the way to Ikom, tried and convicted. To avoid these problems with soldiers on leave it was suggested that they not be allowed to go on leave in uniform and that they should be paid only when they are about to go on leave so that they would have money on them to pay for things rather than seizing them from the people.

Letters Written by Soldiers to the District Officer
Asking for His Assistance

1. NA41463 John Talbot from Besongabang. He worked as a signal man in India. He wrote to the DO on 21 February 1941 asking what was happening to his parents back in Cameroon.

2. NA387549 A/F Jonas Tabe Agbo (4th Battalion of the Nigerian Regiment, West African Force). In a letter he wrote to the DO in Mamfe on 2 September 1942 he asked him to forward 6 pounds 10 shillings he had sent to his sister Madam Hana Maliba of Batoke in Victoria.

3. NA 76695 Martin Abunaw. He served as signal man. He wrote on 9 December 1943 complaining that there were only two of them serving at the station.

4. Ndan Nwanake. This was a letter written by his father, Bawe Tiku, to the DO asking about his son's whereabouts because it had been three years that he had not heard from him.

5. Lucas Ayuk Eyong from Ossing. The DO had written to him on 23 August 1943.

6. James Ako. He wrote to the Mamfe DO requesting to hear from his parents.

7. NA37847 Emmanuel Okon of the 6th Battalion. He wrote to the DO requesting to be able to communicate with his wife.

8. NA205972 Oben Eta. In a letter on 7 April 1944 he asked the DO of Mamfe to check if his father and brother are well. He was serving in the Middle East.

9. Thomas Ayuk from Mamfe wrote on 2 May 1944 to the DO. He was serving in the Middle East.

10. Joseph Tabot from Mamfe serving in the Middle East also wrote to the DO on 14 April 1944.

11. Nicholas Mbekem from Mamfe served in the Middle East. He wrote to the DO of Mamfe on 23 January 1945.

12. The archive had a list of soldiers who had sent money to the DO to be given to their relatives back at home. This was in April 1942: William Kemngo, Lazarus Agbo, David Jang, Stephen Ngora, Manfred Fosimo, Ore Hayi(Eji), and Harry Fiatoh.

Communication between Soldiers on Active Service and Relatives

File No. 905/vol. 1.

File Title: Communication between soldiers on active service and their relatives.

a) NA 387549A/F Jonas Tabe. This soldier sent 6 pounds, 10 pennies to the sister Hana Maliba through DO Mamfe on 2 September 1942.

b) LN16011 John Agbor on 3 October 1943 wrote to the DO complaining that his wife and property left behind had been taken by those who did not join the army. He said that the people at home claimed he had been killed because she received money from the government. They argued that the allotment paid to wives of soldiers was because the soldiers had died.

c) NA16708 Pius Sama in the Middle East on the 13 November 1943 wrote the DO of Mamfe complaing to him that he had not heard from home for a long time.

d) Other soldiers who wrote to the DO Mamfe while at war were:
    Wilson Tambe on 3 December 1943
    Sam Bameta on 4 December 1943
    Peter Tarbe on 19 November 1943 (from Santa Isabel)
    Samuel Okon on 13 December 1943 (from India)
    Bernard Bia on 3 January 1944 (from Middle East)
    Morris Ashu Njok of the 2427 company in the Middle East on 13 January 1944

Bamenda, 1944

The District Officer of Bamenda in his Annual Report for 1944 commented on the loyalty of Division during the war that it "has been good." Out of a large number of men recruited for the fighting and Pioneer services only 44 have been posted as deserters and nine rejoined later. The contribution to the War Relief Week was 2,565 pounds 12sh.

The people failed to raise the quota of rubber demanded of them; but this quota was based on guesswork and took no account of other economic demands. Toward the end of the drive, some people were walking four days trek . . . to find patches of wild rubber and in my opinion this showed as much effort as could be reasonably expected. (See Archive No. Cb1945/1.)

News from Home

Divisional Office Bamenda B 2369
News from the Bamenda Division to Soldiers serving overseas, pp. 3, 4, 20 June 1945, Mogamo Area.

It was reported that the Basel Mission's oldest school near the chief of Batibo had been transferred to Tadkom and raised to elementary Two. In addition four new ones were opened at Bessi, Guzang, Ngai, and one near Mamfe Division.

A short road had been dug from Guzang Market to the main road from Mamfe to Bamenda.

Building construction had not changed as in other areas to sun-dried blocks. Bamboo remained the local material for houses.

In Ashong Enogang had been appointed by the quarter head Niako and now "rules the village justly."

Tegum, the son of Fonjoh, a boy of about 20 years, was ruling the village of Ambo.

Finally, Nwanege, the son of the late Kung, chief of Abeshion (Bessom) succeded his father " and sends greetings."

After the War

There was a letter written on 10 March 1947 relating to some soldiers that were released from the war service. These names appeared as those who were released.

NA38227 L/Corporal Kang Bafuwum. He was then to work as a court messenger.

NA38171 Private Peter Ambe now to work as NA forest guard at Lang.

NA206897 Sergeant M. A. Ngang now to work as 3rd class clerk in the Provincial administration.

News in brief by the DO on 14 December 1945 indicates the arrival of NA103466 J. I. Naseri of Mbonge from India after being there for about four years without coming home and serving in the army. He was received with feasting by relatives and school children.

The District Officer, Bamenda, wrote in his Annual Report for 1946 about returning soldiers to the area (16 January 1947).

He refers to the 1945 Report that a staging camp was ready for returning soldiers but that only one repatriate has ever slept in it and that "they all prefer to proceed immediately to the Abakpa (*refers to a quarter in the town of Bamenda*), but this . . . In consequence, the British non-commissioned officer in charge was withdrawn and the camp abandoned."

The report continues that "there have been no instances of concerted violence by ex-soldiers and little serious crimes . . . but this may follow when their savings are exhausted; these savings are kept as hard cash at the Post Office Bank, deposits made while in the army being withdrawn immediately on their return."

(Most of the archive reports are by Mr. Benard Forkwa, Research Assistant.)

In Closing: A Tribute to Archivist Primus Forgwe

I will be forever grateful for his friendship. My time in Cameroon was immeasurably enriched by the care I received from him. I was lucky to have such a friend.

—Shirley Ardener

Letter from Michael Mom, Bafmeng

Z

№ EX. NA./38215

P6. MICHAEL MOM.

3 MB 9.

The Rev. FATHER   25 – 10 – 88.

BAFMENG – Wum

MENCHUM DIVISION.

REVEREND,

PRESENTATION OF SERVICE
    AWARDS IN THE ARMY.

    I have the honour to present
myself and medals as an ex-Service
army with the above mentioned
numbers.
    I fought the 1939 to 1945
World war in india and Burma
and was awarded 4 medals, two
Gold and 2 Silver namely :-

1 G.R.J. VI The 1939 – 1945 Star (Gold).

2 1939 – 1945 GEORGWS VI D.G BR: The defence
    Medal (Silver).

3 1939 – 1945 GEORGIUS VI D: G. B: OMN: REX ET
    INDIAE: IMP. (Silver).

4 G R J VI The Burma Star (Gold)-
I therefore present Them
as earlier Mentioned in my
letter above.
            I remain,
                Your humble
                    MICHAEL MOM
                    KWR VILLAGE

An Identity Certificate

An example: Thanks to Mrs. Brigitte Nyada, daughter of Joseph Tepe Ndikum.

(This page should be entirely free from erasure)

Final Assessments of Conduct and Character
on leaving the Colours.

Military Conduct... *Very Good*

Testimonial... *This man has served...*

The above assessments have been read to the soldier.

Place... *Enugu*

(Signature & Rank)

Date... *12 Jan 46*

O.C. Unit.

B.C. Headquarter   4NR

Length of Service

Unit	From	To	Years	Days

Service with the Colours showing Transfers (if any).
(Dates to be copied of dates Quarmaster no Strike)

Certificate of Transfer to the Reserve

Date of transfer...

Rank...

Cause of transfer...

Unit from which transferred...

Service with Colours on date of transfer:
...years...days

Description of Soldier on transfer.

Age... Height... ft... ins.

Marks or Scars...

(Signature & Rank)

Place...

Date...

O.i/c Records

PARTICULARS ON DISCHARGE   Triplicate

NIGERIA ... RECORDS

Disability Awards.
(a) Pension of £ s. d. per mensem.
(b) Gratuity £ s. d.
School Educational Standard on Joining Army:—
(eg. Standard I)... *Nil*

Education
Courses attended in Army... (Yrs)

Qualified for "P" badge NOT APPLICABLE
Simple Spoken English (Yes or No)... *No*
Literate in English (Yes or No)... *No*
Literate in Hausa (Yes or No)... *No*
Literate in... (Yes or No)... *No*
Trade or Occupation on joining the Army... *DRIVER*

Present Army Trade and classification thereof:

Any additional Trade in which classified while serving... *Nil*

Any other Industrial skill acquired while serving... *Nil*

An Anglican Church in Burma

- **Anglican Church in Burma**
- 1940   World War II came into Burma, and foreign missionaries had to depart from the country.
- 1941   In January, the Japanese army crossed the Sanlwin River came and into Burma and the Kappli mission was disconnected with Rangoon. Because of the severe attack of the Japanese army, all missionaries and foreign civilians including their families moved to upper Burma.
- 1942   George Appleton was appointed archdeacon by Bishop George A. West to look after the mission of Burma from India. Since Burma was occupied by the Japanese, all mission works including missionary schools and hospitals were stopped and most native Anglicans dispersed. The native clergy and ministers risked their lives in serving among those dispersed Anglicans in that difficult and dangerous period. Many native martyrs appeared in that period.
- 1945   In July, West returned from abroad and stayed in Rangoon.
- 1946   To reorganize the church, West created three archdeaconries, one for Delta, one for Mandalay, and one for Toungoo. These posts were filled by national clergy, Luke Po Kun, J. Aung Hla, and Ah Mya, respectively. Holy Cross College was reopened by R. W. Garrad.

[George Appleton, Archdeacon of Rangoon, *The War and After, Burma* (London: Society for the Propagation of the Gospel, ca. 1946). Project Canterbury. Dedication: To the memory of Ma Pwa Sein, a great Christian woman.]

Four Medals Awarded to Some of the Ex-soldiers

The *Burma Star* was awarded to British and Commonwealth forces who served in the Burma Campaign from 1941 to 1945, during World War II.

The *War Medal 1939–1945* is a campaign medal awarded to citizens of the Commonwealth who had served full-time in the Armed Forces or the Merchant Navy for at least 28 days between 3 September 1939 and 2 September 1945 during the war.

The *Defence Medal* was awarded to citizens of the British Commonwealth for both military and certain types of civilian war service during World War II.

The *Africa Star* is a medal awarded to British and Commonwealth forces who served in North Africa between 10 June 1940 and 12 May 1943 during World War II.

Professor Graham W. Irwin, 1920–1991

This book is dedicated to the memory of Professor Graham Irwin, who was a friend and teacher.

The *New York Times,* on October 16th, reported his death under the headline: Graham W. Irwin, Historian, 71. The brief article began: "Graham W. Irwin, an historian of Africa who directed Columbia University's African Institute from 1974 to 1983, died on Saturday at his home in Manhattan. He was 71 years old."

Columbia University had a longer piece reported in the *Columbia University Record* for October 25, 1991. It is reproduced here.

IN MEMORIAM: Graham W. Irwin

from the *Columbia University Record*, October 25, 1991

Graham W. Irwin, an authority on West African precolonial history, a professor and administrator at Columbia University for 28 years, and one-time Executive Secretary of the ASA, died October 12 of cancer at his Manhattan home. He was 71 years old.

Until his illness last spring, he had taught courses on West African history, economics, diplomacy, and culture and in the undergraduate core curriculum in Columbia College. He joined the Columbia faculty in 1963 as associate professor, was promoted to professor in 1965, and named professor emeritus in 1988, continuing to teach part-time as a special research scholar.

His interest in African history dated from his appointment in 1958 to the History Department at the newly formed University of Ghana in Accra. According to his colleague, Columbia history professor Marcia Wright, he had been hired to teach European colonialism and, surrounded by historians of Africa, he developed his interest in the Ashanti people and their diplomatic history. His research focused on the precolonial history of West Africa in the 18th and 19th centuries, particularly the Gold Coast, now Ghana.

He also studied the Black African Diaspora and was the author of *Africans Abroad: A Documentary History of the Black Diaspora in Asia, Latin America, and the Caribbean During the Age of Slavery* (Columbia University Press, 1977) and *Nineteenth Century Borneo: A Study in Diplomatic Rivalry* (The Hague: Martinus Nijhoff, 1955). He was a pioneer in the sixties in teaching of African history and the Diaspora and in 1973 wrote *The African Experience Outside Africa,* which was published by Columbia College and used in the core curriculum.

With Columbia historian Richard B. Morris, a scholar of American colonial and constitutional history, he edited the *Harper Encyclopedia of the Modern World* (Harper & Row, 1971).

He is survived by his wife of 35 years, Jane T. N. Irwin, and a stepson, Julian K. Wheatley of Ithaca, NY.

Friends wishing to make donations in memory of Graham Irwin may send them to the Africana Library Fund, 314 B Butler Library, Columbia University, New York, NY 10027.

Another tribute was in the Newsletter of the Institute of African Studies at Columbia in February 1992. The director at the time, Professor George Bond, wrote that "The Institute deeply regrets the death of Professor Graham Irwin whose profound concern for Africa will be difficult to equal." Professor Bond pointed out that Graham Irwin had been vice dean of the School of International and Public Affairs (1983–1988) and also Director of the Institute of African Studies (1974–1983). "Professor Irwin led a rich and productive life as a distinguished historian who chose Asia and West Africa as the central regions on which to exercise his remarkable talents." On December 11, 1991, there was a memorial service in St Paul's Chapel on Columbia's campus.

Photo courtesy of
Mrs. Marlyse Rand

Mrs. Marlyse Rand was the secretary of the Institute of African Studies from its beginnings for many years. She helped to piece together Graham Irwin's Australian roots.

Graham Wilkie Irwin was born on 12 October 1920 in Adelaide, South Australia. His home town was College Park, Norwood Payneham St. Peters near Adelaide. He was the son of Rev. William Henry Irwin, who taught at St. Peters College in Adelaide, and Edith Morris, formerly head mistress of Melbourne Girls Grammar School. Her father was the Registrar of the Church.

Graham enlisted in the Australian army during World War II on 22 March 1941. He served in the Australian Light Horse 2nd/9th Armored Regiment, rising to the rank of Captain. The Regiment took part in action against the Japanese in Borneo, Dutch East Indies, in 1945. The 9th Regiment received three battle honors for its service in World War II.

Graham Irwin had an older brother, William Morris Irwin (1914–1994), who also served in World War II. He was a medical doctor who rose to be a Lieutenant Colonel in the Medical Corps. He was in Palestine and Syria during 1941 and 1942 and later in the Pacific islands.

After the War he studied for a BA at Adelaide University in 1946 and then went to the UK and Cambridge University where he had another BA in 1949 and an MA and PhD in 1953. His dissertation was on nineteenth-century Borneo, the place where he had served in the War. It was published as a book in 1955.

Charles Donald Cowan, professor of South East Asian history and later director of SOAS in London wrote of the book: "The whole of the story is admirably recounted by Dr. Irwin. One of the merits of his book is that he is the first historian, British or Dutch, to make extensive use of both British and Dutch archives in this field, so that his treatment of the subject is both exhaustive and well balanced. . . . Another is the vigorous and attractive language in which he clothes his scholarship."

From 1953 to 1956 he was a history lecturer at the University of Malaya. From there he returned to Australia as a lecturer in history at the University of Sydney. There he taught the history of Southeast Asia, China, Japan, and Java.

Marlyse Rand passed on two photographs of Professor Irwin soon after his death. One was him at his desk at Columbia University and the other was of him in Ghana where he took up a post at the University of Ghana in 1958.

Professor Bond wrote that Graham Irwin "began his association with Africa when he assumed the post of senior lecturer in history at the University of Ghana. During his five years in Ghana he became a professor and head of the University's History Department, as well as Chairman of the Board of the Faculty of Arts and Pro-Vice Chancellor

It was his time in Ghana that helped lead Professor Irwin into African history and administration. Marcia Wright writes about the influence of those years in his In Memoriam.

Ghana 1959: Staff and Students, Akuafo Hall, Ghana Academy of Learning. Graham Irwin, seated center.
Photo courtesy of Mrs. Marlyse Rand

Additional information about life at the new University in Ghana was found in an article by David Levering Lewis in the *American Scholar* for Winter 1999, titled "Ghana, 1963: A Memoir." One of the people who welcomed David Lewis to Accra was Graham Irwin.

Lewis, an American historian, is now professor emeritus of history at New York University. He is twice winner of a Pulitzer Prize for part one and part two of his biography of W. E. B. Du Bois.

Akuafo Hall, where Professor Irwin was, also known as the "Hall of Excellence," was the second residence hall in the University College of the Gold Coast. Founded by Kwame Nkrumah as the Ghana Academy of Learning, it was opened by Prince Philip on 27 November 1959. Later it became the Ghana

Academy of Arts and Science in 1961. It was the first institution of its kind in post- independence Africa.

In 1963 he left Ghana and came to Columbia University as an associate professor, and then, in 1965, he became a professor. "During the 1960s he brought to Columbia College a strong interest in African History and the Diaspora." These themes were taken up in two of his books: *The African Experience* and *Outside Africa.*

The best tribute are the final words of Professor Bond:

> *Professor Irwin was a masterful teacher, a compassionate examiner and a true guardian of scholarly standards. He was a defender of the rights of African students and insisted that all students should be evaluated according to the same academic criteria of excellence. His commitment to knowledge and teaching transcended his formal requirement. He continued . . . to think of ways of extending the minds of his students. After 28 years of service to Columbia University and African studies, the intelligent scholarship, the inspired and compassionate teaching and the administrative wisdom of this quiet and gentle man will be missed. . . .*

It was Professor Irwin who opened the door for me to pursue African History in 1981. His words were also the incentive to carry on with oral history following a dissertation in 1987. He referred to all the interviews quoted as "splendid sources." That was enough, since it came from him, to lead to this book so many years later.

Notes

Preface

1. David Killingray, *Fighting for Britain, African Soldiers in the Second World War* (Rochester, NY: James Currey, 2012), 260. From the back cover of Killingray's book: "During the Second World War over half-a-million African troops served with the British Army as combatants and non-combatants in the Horn of Africa, the Middle East, Italy and Burma—the largest single movement of African men overseas since the slave trade."

Introduction

1. Barnaby Phillips, *Another Man's War: The Story of a Burma Boy in Britain's Forgotten Army* (London: Oneworld, 2014), 313 pages. Phillips tells the story of the survival of Isaac Fadoyebo, a Nigerian soldier who was part of the African army that fought in Burma for the British in the Second World War.

2. John A. L. Hamilton, *War Bush: 81 (West African) Division in Burma, 1943–1945* (Norwich: Michael Russell, 2001).

3. Anthony Ndi, "The Second World War in Southern Cameroon and Its Impact on Mission-State Relations, 1939–50," in *Africa and the Second World War*, ed. David Killingray and Richard Rathbone (London: Macmillan, 1986), 204–31.

4. David Killingray, *Fighting for Britain, African Soldiers in the Second World War* (Rochester, NY: James Currey, 2012), 289.

Chapter 1. British Cameroons: 1916–1939

1. David E. Gardinier, "The British in Cameroons, 1919–1939," in *Germany and Britain in Africa*, ed. P. G. Gifford and W. R. Levine (New Haven, CT: Yale University Press, 1967), 513–35.

2. Hamilton, *War Bush*, 22.

3. R. Reese, Department of Veterans Affairs, Opinion, *New York Times*, 31 May 2021.

4. Judith A. Byfield, "Preface," in *Africa and World War II*, ed. Judith A. Byfield, Carolyn A. Brown, Timothy Parsons, and Ahmad Alawad Sikainga (Cambridge: Cambridge University Press, 2015), xvii.

5. Sarah Pruitt, "How the Treaty of Versailles and German Guilt Led to World War Two, Wilson's idealistic vision, Versailles Peace Conference, " History, A & E Television Networks, https://www.history.com/news/treaty-of-versailles-world-war-ii-german-guilt-effects, 29 June 1918, updated 29 June 2023.

6. During World War I the German colony of Kamerun was occupied by British, French, and Belgium troops, and later under a League of Nations Mandate by Great Britain and France. The British territory was administered as Northern and Southern Cameroons. Northern Cameroons consisted of two noncontiguous sections, divided by a point where the Nigerian and

French Cameroun borders met. In the 1930s, most of the white population consisted of Germans, who were interned starting in June 1940. The native population of 400,000 showed little interest in volunteering for the British forces; only 3,500 men did so. See George N. Njung, "The British Cameroons Mandate Regime: The Roots of the Twenty-First-Century Political Crisis in Cameroon," *American Historical Review* 124.5 (2019): 1715–22.

7. Robert O'Neil, "A History of Moghamo, 1865–1940, Authority and Change in a Cameroon Grassfields Culture" (PhD thesis, Columbia University, 1987), 192ff.; Elizabeth Chilver, "Native Administration in West Central Cameroons, 1902–1954, in *Essays in Imperial Government: Presented to Margery Perham*, ed. Kenneth Robinson and Frederick Madden (Oxford: Blackwell, 1963), 109.

8. Sanford H. Bederman, *The Cameroons Development Corporation: Partner in National Growth* (Bota, West Cameroon: Cameroons Development Corp., 1968), 16–17.

9. Gardinier, "The British in Cameroons," 547–51.

10. Victor T. LeVine, *The Cameroons from Mandate to Independence* (Berkeley: UCLA Press, 1964), 125.

11. Malcolm Milne, *No Telephone to Heaven: From Apex to Nadir—Colonial Service in Nigeria Aden, the Cameroons, and the Gold Coast, 1938–61* (Stockbridge, Longstock, UK: Meon Hill Press, 1999) 464 pages. The reviewer took the quote of Dr. Anyaoku from the *Times Literary Supplement* (TLS) for 12 May 2000.

12. Sir Bryan Sharwood Smith, *Recollections of British Administration in the Cameroons and Northern Nigeria 1921–1957: "But Always as Friends"* (London: George Allen & Unwin; Durham, NC: Duke University Press, 1969), 460 pages.

13. Sharwood-Smith, *Recollections of British Administration*, 22.

14. Gardinier, *Cameroon,* 549.

15. O'Neil, "History of Moghamo," 280ff.

16. O'Neil, "History of Moghamo," 8.

17. Robert O'Neil, *Mission to the British Cameroons* (London: Mission Book Service, 1991), 27.

18. O'Neil, *Mission to the British Cameroons*, 61ff., 82.

19. Thomas Mulligan, unpublished Ms, "MHM in Cameroon," MHA, ca. 1972.

20. Charles W. Weber, *International Influences and Baptist Mission in West Cameroon: German-American Missionary Endeavor under International Mandate and British Colonialism* (Leiden: Brill Academic, 1993), especially 32, 126.

21. See Carl F. H. Henry, *Bender in the Cameroons: The Story of Missionary Triumph in a Dark Region of the World's Darkest Continent* (Cleveland, OH: Roger Williams Press, 1940).

22. Werner Keller, *The History of the Presbyterian Church in West Cameroon* (Victoria: Presbook, 1969), 66.

23. Anthony Ndi, *Mill Hill Missionaries in the Southern West Cameroon: 1922–1972: Prime Partners in Nation Building* (Nairobi: Pauline Publications Africa, 2005), 94ff.

24. LeVine, *The Cameroons*, 121, 130.

25. Ndi, "The Second World War and Southern Cameroons," 204ff.

Chapter 2. World War II and
the Royal West African Air Force

1. David Killingray, *Fighting for Britain, African Soldiers in the Second World War* (Suffolk: James Currey, 2012), 7–9.

2. Killingray, *Fighting for Britain*, 7.

3. Killingray, *Fighting for Britain*, 31–32.

4. See Nowa Omoigui, *Barracks: The History behind Those Names-Part 5*, DAWODU. COM. "In Burma, from 1943–45, as part of the 81st and 82nd West African Divisions, the Nigeria Regiment of the West African Frontier Force also fought in North Arakan, Kaladan, Mayu Valley, Myohaung, Arakan Beaches, Kangaw, Dalet and Tamandu and was a component of Chindit operations in 1944. The high point of the Nigerian regiment in Burma was the fall of Myohaung on January 24–25, 1945. Before independence, January 25 used to be celebrated annually in Nigeria as an official military day."

Chapter 3. Recruitment

1. John Bull, *Palm Oil Chop: A West African Dish of Many Ingredients: Sierra Leone, British Cameroons, India, Burma, The Journal of a White West African in Colonial Days*, Part 2: *The War Years: West Africa, India, Burma* (Pietermaritzburg, 1987) (quoted in Hamilton, *War Bush*, 380).

2. Phillips, *Another Man's War*, 5.

3. Philips, *Another Man's War*, 17.

4. Secretary of State Enugu, Buea Archive, 1939.

5. *New York Times*, 1 April 2000.

6. Correspondence, John Hamilton, 10 May, 2000, Leatherhead, Surrey. Also, from East Africa Raphael Chikukwa, from Zimbabwe, tracked down ten veterans in Zambia, Tanzania and his home country. His article was published in the *Guardian* for 3 September 2006. According to Chikukwa, Britain's recruiting policies were more sophisticated than they had been in World War I. "Anti-fascists propaganda used the radio and newspapers to reach the population. Cartoons and drawings were used in the papers and on posters proposing what life might be like under German rule. Some felt that the cause was a just cause but that they were later betrayed" (*Guardian*, 3 September 2006).

7. Myron Echenberg, *Colonial Conscripts: The Tirailleurs Sénégalais in French West Africa, 1857–1960*, Social History of Africa (Portsmouth, NH: Heinemann, 1991), 75, 88, 90–91.

8. Killingray, *Fighting for Britain*, 37–47, 75. See also notes on Buea Archives in Appendix 2, p. 120.

9. Marika Sherwood, *World War II: Colonies, Colonials* (London: Savannah Press, 2013).

10. Oliver Coates, "New Perspectives on West Africa and World War Two," *Journal of African Military History* 4.1–2 (2020): 5–39.

11. Coates, "New Perspectives on West Africa," abstract.

12. See Ndi, "The Second World War and Southern Cameroons," 204–31.

13. Buea Archive.

Chapter 4. Deployment to North Africa and Burma

1. Naval History Homepage, *Campaign Summaries of World War II, Indian Ocean and SE Asia including Burma, 1943–45*.

Chapter 5. North Africa

1. Killingray, *Fighting for Britain*, 7–8.

2. Timothy Parsons, "The Military Experiences of Ordinary Africans in World War II," in *Africa and World War II*, ed. Byfield, 8.

3. Australian War Memorial, Italian POWs; 5 September 2016, Damian Lucjan, Guest Author, War History online.

4. Chris Day, "The Forgotten Army: West African Troops in Burma, 1945," National

Archives, 12 August 2020, https://blog.nationalarchives.gov.uk/the-forgotten-army-west-african-troops-in-burma-1945/.

Chapter 6. Burma

1. Henry Maule, *Spearhead General: The Epic Story of General Sir Frank Messervy and His Men in Eritrea, North Africa and Burma* (London: Odhams, 1961), 215.

2. Phillips, *Another Man's War*, cover.

3. David Killingray, "The Idea of a British Imperial African Army," *Journal of African History* 20.3 (1979): 421–36, here 432. On 30 December, chiefs of staff agreed that West African troops could serve outside of Africa by June 1943. From 1943 to the end of the war about 120,000 African troops arrived in Ceylon. See also p. 433n. 65: 72,290 West Africans served in Asia; 16,472 in the Mideast; 56,100 in Africa.

4. Nancy Ellen Lawler, *Soldiers, Airmen, Spies, and Whisperers: The Gold Coast in World War II* (Athens: Ohio University Press, 2002), 228. General Gifford flew to India to become GOC in charge of Eastern Army.... 81st arrived Aug/Sept 1943; 82nd Division left January 1944.

5. T. R. Moreman, *The Jungle, Japanese and the British Commonwealth Armies at War 1941–45* (London: Frank Cass, 2005), 89: The 81st West African Division landed at Bombay and moved into jungle camps near Chas and later the Western Ghats to undergo badly needed collective training. The first test of battle came at Arakan, when brigades of the 81st (WA) Division under Major General Woolner "provided distant flank protection operating on a very light scale of equipment and supplied from the air."

6. Milne, *No Telephone to Heaven*, 97, 99–100. "…Peter Stallard. He was a Northern Region ADO, two years my senior, tall, thin and very committed. He was to have a distinguished war ending up as a Lieut Colonel with the eighty first division in Burma. In 1957 he was in Lagos as secretary to Abubakar Tefewa Balewa, first premier of the Federation of Nigeria."

7. Omoigui, *Barracka,* DAWODU.com. "It is in commemoration of these heroic battles of the Second World War that, for example, MARDA BARRACKS IN LAGOS; LETMAUK BARRACKS IN IBADAN; DALET, MOGADISHU, COLITO AND KALAPANZIN BARRACKS IN KADUNA; AND THE CHINDIT BARRACKS IN ZARIA are named."

8. The account is from Phillips, *Another Man's War,* 44–48, 52, 69, 74.

Chapter 7. Interviews with Ex-Servicemen

1. Bilad Kaggia, *Roots of Freedom, 1921–1963: The Autobiography of Bilad Kaggia* (Nairobi, 1975); quoted in Killingray, *Fighting for Britain*, 107: Killingray also writes that a small booklet titled *Walks around Jerusalem* was given to literate troops. A foreword stated: "This book is a gift to you from the Middle East Forces so that you may learn about all the wonderful places which you will see, and so that you may remember them."

2. On his visit to the United States in 1996, Mr. Joseph Ndikum paid a visit to a friend who had an interest in the author's mission in Cameroon. Somewhere there is a photograph of Mr. Ndikum in full uniform shaking hands with John D. Lambert at his home in Fairfield, Connecticut. John graduated from Fairfield University in 1998 with a degree in English and History. He passed away in 2000, taken by complications from muscular dystrophy.

Chapter 8. Chaplains

1. Mill Hill Chaplain, "Faith in Wartime," *Missions and Missionaries* (Spring 1947): 10.

2. O'Neil, *Mission to the British Cameroons*, 82.

3. Pius Mbasong, Gungong, 8 August 1988.

4. Mill Hill Archive

5. Mill Hill Archive.

6. Tom Johnstone and James Hagerty, *The Cross and the Sword: Catholic Chaplains in the Armed Forces* (London: Geoffrey Chapman, 1995), 204–9.

7. Johnstone and Hagerty, *Cross and the Sword*, 253–58.

8. George Appleton, *The War and After, Burma* (London: Society for the Propagation of the Gospel, c. 1946), section [29/30].

Chapter 9. Thanksgiving in Rangoon and Return to West Africa, 1945, 1946s

1. Hamilton, *War Bush,* 369.

2. "Rededication of Rangoon's Defiled Anglican Cathedral", London, July 29, published in the *Sydney Morning Herald*, Monday, 30 July 1945.

3. Phillips, *Another Man's War*, 165.

Chapter 10. Remembrance Day in Bota Gardens, 1999

1. An invitation came from Mr. D. Scott of the CDC. We met on a return flight to the UK and USA in November 1999. Born in 1937 in Hull, he completed his GCE and joined the army. He was sent to Sandhurst and was later stationed in Malaysia. He has worked in India, Hong Kong, and Australia and was on a plantation in Assam for eighteen years. Mr. Scott was also in Papua New Guinea. In Cameroon he was first at Ngu and then Misonga.

Appendix 2. World War II and the British Cameroons from the Buea Archives

1. See Jacqueline-Bethel Tchouta Mougoué, "Buea Archives," https://jacquelinebethel mougoue.com/buea-archives.

Index

About the Author

Robert O'Neil, a priest and member of the Mill Hill Missionaries, was born in Bridgeport, Connecticut, USA. He holds a PhD in History from Columbia University in New York. Ordained in July 1965 at Westminster Cathedral by Cardinal Heenan, he spent his first years on mission in Cameroon, West Africa. He is the author of *Cardinal Herbert Vaughan, Mission to the British Cameroons, Mission to the Upper Nile,* and *Born Under the Gun.* For nineteen years he was an assistant at St. Mary's Parish on the Lower East Side of Manhattan. He resides at the Mill Hill residence in Hartsdale, New York.

About the Publisher

The Crossroad Publishing Company publishes Crossroad and Herder & Herder books. We offer a 200-year global family tradition of books on spiritual living and religious thought. We promote reading as a time-tested discipline for focus and understanding. We help authors shape, clarify, write, and effectively promote their ideas. We select, edit, and distribute books. With our expertise and passion, we provide wholesome spiritual nourishment for heart, mind, and soul through the written word.

Praise for
No Small Thing

The history of the participation of Cameroonians, voluntarily, and at times forcefully conscripted, into a war they knew nothing about, much less benefit from, cannot be constructed exclusively from official archival documents. This excellent and easy-to-read written account of some Cameroonian ex-servicemen who assisted the British army in far-off lands in defeating the enemies is commendable. These ex-servicemen have told their stories through the author.

The title, *No Small Thing*, taken from the account of one of the principal ex-servicemen, Joseph Tepe Ndikum, aptly tells the story of how ordinary Cameroonians, some with no formal education, contributed, in no small way, in the victory of the Allies in the Second World War. Sadly, these ex-servicemen were not adequately rewarded. History and the families of these brave men should be grateful to the author, Robert J. O'Neil, for having brilliantly weaved together the experiences of these men in a deadly encounter which they went into, some without hesitation, not knowing the risks and outcome.

Professor Victor Julius Ngoh
Historian, University of Yaounde (Retired), Fulbright Scholar
Author of *Southern Cameroons, 1922-1961,*
A Constitutional History (2001)
History of a People, Cameroon 1884-Present(2019)

www.ingramcontent.com/pod-product-compliance
Lightning Source LLC
Chambersburg PA
CBHW021332090426
42742CB00008B/577